SUMMER PROGRAM

TIPS, STRATEGIES &

ACTIVITIES

FOR SCHOOL-AGERS 5- 14 YEARS-OLD

Articles and Activities
from the
School-Age NOTES Newsletter

Edited by Rich Scofield

School-Age NOTES ● Nashville, Tennessee

PUBLISHED BY:

School-Age NOTES
P.O. Box 40205
Nashville TN 37204

1-800-410-8780
615-279-0700

www.schoolagenotes.com

Photo credits:
page 9: courtesy of Girls, Inc. of Holyoke MA
pages 17, 54: courtesy of Women's Community Y, Leavenworth, KS
page 26: courtesy of Jericho Kids Club, Vancouver, British Columbia
pages 31, 87: courtesy of YMCA McHenry Co., Crystal Lakes IL
page 34: courtesy of Jupiter Elementary School After-School Program, Jupiter FL
page 47: courtesy of Findlay After & Before School Sessions, Findlay OH
page 48: Nancy Alexander
pages 61, 81, 107: courtesy of Foundation Kid Connect, Ralston NE
page 108: courtesy of Letterkenny Army Depot School-Age Services, Chambersburg PA

10 9 8 7 6 5 4 3 2

ISBN: 0-917505-15-8

WHAT'S INSIDE

A NOTE FROM THE PUBLISHER

"Kids will be looking for fun, friendship, and not too much pressure to succeed."
– *Kathy Hermes*, p. 20

"School-age child care in the summer differs greatly from the rest of the year."
– *Rich Scofield*, p. 5

"Summer programs need individuals who can pace and sustain themselves for the whole day."
– *Linda Eisele*, p. 24

"You can't have a successful program that starts with piecemeal planning."
– *Linda Sisson*, p. 18

"Parents will not be satisfied with the program if you do not deliver what they expected."
– *Kathy Hermes*, p. 21

"It is not essential for every camper to be doing something all the time. The nicest gift we can give to some children is the opportunity to be still and do nothing; the finest thing we can teach them is to take time to STOP, LOOK and LISTEN."
– *Grace Mitchell, 1961*, p. 36

"It is impossible to run the program and plan it at the same time."
– *Joan Walker*, p. 28

These quotes give both a glimpse of planning a summer program and understate what it takes to run a good program. The articles and ideas selected for this book are as valid today as when they were originally published.

When I started School-Age NOTES in 1980, I had in mind a newsletter that would have short articles, tips and strategies—"notes"—about school-age child care, as well as activities. There have been tremendous changes in the field since then. At that time, there was no money for training and technical assistance and little for subsidized slots. Now there is $1.3 billion proposed in federal spending, a national accreditation system, and in the planning stages, a national credential for school-age workers. What we call the field has gone from "school-age child care" to "school-age care" to "out-of-school time" to "after-school programs."

However, our newsletter has essentially stayed the same—"notes." These tips, ideas and strategies are not only about before- and after-school and full days, but also about summer. Every year for 20 years, interspersed across the newsletter from January through August issues, we have had "notes" about summer programs.

This book is a compilation of the best ideas, plus activities, from those 20 years. As a reminder when reading, the articles are as they were originally published and have not been updated. The articles do not reference the current state of people, or organizations, or availablility of resources. Some things will appear dated (i.e. record players), names change, and organizations go out of business or change names.

May this help you with your summer program and, as we stated in our first brochure in 1980, "help you to help the school-age child to learn, grow, be responsible, and have fun."

Rich Scofield
Editor/Publisher

SUMMER PROGRAM GUIDELINES: A GENERAL INTRODUCTION

School-age child care in the summer differs greatly from the rest of the year. Free play and activity centers, often the core of after-school programming, aren't enough for the long days and weeks of summer. This is a time when more involved activities and long-range projects are needed. Changing the environment by rearranging the classroom and setting up new interest centers will help the children make the transition from after-school care to all-day care. The following is information which may be helpful.

Programming Ideas

Themes

Themes can help spark creativity planning, especially when the children are (as they should be) doing the planning. Goals can be set, themes can be created. Activities, trips and events related to the themes can be planned. Books and films related to these can be borrowed from the library. Examples:

- Photography
- Vegetable Dyeing
- Mexican Crafts

Badges

A badge system can help keep children motivated and interested during the summer and help them set long-and short-term goals. Different levels to each badge will accommodate the wide age range and level of ability found in a typical school-age group. Work to earn badges can be done during planned activity time. To begin:

1). Plan kinds of badges children can earn.

2). Plan list of activities necessary to each badge.

3). Plan activities to help children earn badges.

Workshops

The following can be done on a weekly basis and can be provided by teachers (staff) or volunteers (experts) from the community: sewing, wrestling, dancing, karate, swimming, nutrition.

Gardening - planning the garden, digging and sowing seeds, weeding, watering and cooking grown produce.

Cooking - including planning, shopping, preparing, eating, and clean-up.

Scouting - Boy Scouts, Girl Scouts, Cub Scouts and Brownies.

Special Activities

— Marathon games (Monopoly™, etc.)

— Tournaments (pool, checkers, backgammon, jumping rope, hula-hooping)

— Indoor skating

— "Snow ball" fights with yarn balls

— Newsletters the children make themselves

— Mechanical junk box (broken appliances with cords removed)

— Visiting children at other centers

— Visiting elderly at senior citizen centers

Getting Out in the Community

Ideas for field trips: parks, historical sites, businesses, factories, bakeries, bottling plants, fast food restaurants, police and fire departments, airport, post office, local tourist attractions (the places local residents never go to see).

Most give school group tours, some provide free samples. If unfamiliar with community, call park department, other centers or local principals for ideas.

Bringing the Community In

Many professionals are willing to come in and explain and demonstrate to a group their particular area of expertise. Parents are a good source! Examples: dancers, police, firefighters, postmen, sculptors, puppeteers, theatre groups, potters, dentists, etc.

Fundraising

Money and earning money is attractive to all school-age children, but especially the older ones. Be sure to have a goal to the fundraising, an end result, which could be a major event (camping trip, a day trip out of town) or something smaller (a new kickball or trip to the movies).

Ideas: car wash, bake sales, pancake breakfasts, plays, magic and puppet shows, collecting newspapers and cans.

Job Opportunities

Jobs can be a wonderful experience for young children. Start with applications and interviews. Use schedules and time cards. Provide compensation, if not money then non-sugar treats or rewards, e.g. extra time at the park, in the pool, etc.

Ideas for Jobs: cooking, cleaning, office chores, repairs, yardwork, putting away supplies, caring for a younger child.

Space

Space and time to be alone is essential in a summer program. Children need time alone especially considering they are usually in a group with about 20 other children for a good part of the day. Spread them out so they have more room. Relieve overcrowding during meals, in bathrooms, on vans and buses, etc. Use spillover space in hallways and sidewalks to lessen the number of people in one area and the noise level. Establish definite rules about respecting others personal belongings. Plan time for the children to be alone and in small groups. Break up space as much as possible with bookshelves or dividers. Provide lots of ways of making hide-away places such as blankets over tables and empty furniture or large appliance boxes. Use alcoves, closets, cloakrooms.

Rest Time

One hour is the normal resting time for school-agers, anything over that should be voluntary. Have plenty of cots, mats, pillows, blankets and sheets on hand. Some alternatives to napping and lying still are:

- listening to homemade story tape
- rubbing preschool or toddler backs (if program includes them)
- one child reading aloud to the rest of the children
- reading books (have a summer reading contest)
- resting outdoors under a tree

Administration

Staffing

Changes in staff schedules are common in school-age care. Summer calls for full time 8 hour a day positions instead of split shifts. If there's no money in the budget for this, look for volunteers from the school system, secretaries, teachers, older children, etc. — who have the summer off. If hiring extra temporary help, look for college students or teacher aides. Extra time for planning and staff meetings will have to be scheduled.

Transportation

Transportation can be a big problem but here are some ideas that may help: Use public buses, staff cars, trains, or taxis, ask parent or volunteers to drive, rent vans. Ask a church or company with bus or van to donate or loan vehicle. Walk — explore the neighborhood. Borrow vehicle from a social service agency. If it's a matter of overcrowding, plan shorter trips and take 2 loads.

Summer Safety

In order to provide a safe summer program, the staff and children need to know the safety rules and procedures.

- Develop guidelines for playground
- Post chart of emergency treatment
- Emergency numbers posted by phone
- Put together First-Aid kit
- Post copy of treatment for insect bites and stings
- Have at least one staff person trained in CPR
- Provide workshops for staff

Food

An all day program means lunch besides the regular snacks. Who will be cooking? Will the children bring their own lunches? Is there a box lunch program or summer lunch funds in your community? If children will be bringing their lunches, provide parents with information on nutritious sack lunchs. If the center will be serving lunch remember to have plenty of fruits, salads and cold soups, and second helpings for all. An active summer program can work up a powerful appetite. If overcrowding is a problem, arrange for the children to eat in shifts.

Extra Clothes

Be sure each child has an extra set of weather-appropriate clothes at school for those unexpected spills and falls in the mud. A swimsuit and towel will be necessary if swimming or water experiences will be part of the program. Try to arrange a place where these items can hang to dry. Clothes should be labeled, but if they're not, a good activity can be for the children to label their own.

SUMMER SCENE

When children arrive at the program, they've already had a few hours of living with their families which has created feelings—sad, happy, angry, guilty, excited—that spill over into the school-age program. The caregiver's greeting of "Good morning, Joel," and the caregiver's quick "tuning-in" to how Joel is as he comes through the door makes a difference in Joel's smooth transition from home to program.

Summer allows for long stretches where children can feel as though a particular piece of equipment is all theirs. During the shorter hours after school there never seems to be enough time. Providing many choices of activities helps facilitate longer periods of use per child.

Small groups of children eating together at lunch offers opportunities to talk, to share, to build friendships. It also decreases the chances of out of bound behavior, which can occur more easily in large groups of children.

Up very early, most school-agers need a chance to let their bodies rest and unwind. This also helps prevent activity levels from spiraling upward and out of control.

Note: Sometimes 15-30 minutes in vigorous physical activity after lunch and before quiet time helps children appreciate this recouping and unwinding time.

Summer provides more hours for outdoor play. It's a great time to inject new energy into your program by bringing indoor type activities outside: blocks, painting, crafts, table games, even sit-down group discussions.

Going home after a long but fun-filled day.

GETTING READY FOR SUMMER

READINESS CHECKLIST FOR SUMMER

☐ Brainstorm goals — both individual and group goals for your children.

☐ Contact local parks, museums, tourist attractions, swimming areas, etc. for information on what's available, when, costs, and any discounts for groups.

☐ Sit down with children and ask them what they want to do.

☐ Plan one or several themes for the summer to help add continuity to planning and activities.

☐ Send out a newsletter to parents to announce what the summer program will be like, special themes, events, trips, etc.

☐ Notify parents about any extra fees for field trips, materials, etc.

☐ If sack lunches will be necessary, let parents know what, when and some ideas on appropriate items to include and those to keep at home (e.g. bottles, perishables).

☐ First Aid box is re-supplied.

☐ Develop traveling first aid kit for trips, walks to the parks, etc.

☐ Brief staff on emergency procedures (e.g fire drill) and day to day summer procedures to all children. Make sure new kids are aware of all regular rules and procedures.

☐ Update emergency phone number and medical information on children and staff.

☐ Prepare environment (re-arrange old activity centers, develop new ones, gather rest-time equipment).

☐ Schedule teachers' and children's day.

☐ Arrange transportation and food.

RATE YOUR SUMMER PROGRAM

❑   Can the children plan and carry out long-term projects?

❑   Do the children have adult help when needed but can carry out projects with some degree of independence and privacy?

❑   Do the children have opportunities to test the limits of their skills and strengths in activities that have a small element of risk, such as climbing trees, taking hikes, and building fires?

❑   Can children choose to do real work around the center like painting or making minor repairs?

❑   Do the children find a large variety of games in the center?

❑   Can the children select games and activities they like, and ask and get good suggestions from caregivers as needed?

❑   Are caregivers or other adults available to show "how to" and teach interesting skills?

❑   Are activities offered that use special tools, such as woodworking and pottery?

❑   Are there opportunities to leave the center and explore the community with caregivers or to swim, bowl or participate in other activities?

❑   Are there opportunities for the children to earn money by doing chores in the community?

❑   Are there times for the children to be left on their own to find their own solutions to the "there's nothing to do" problem?

❑   Are there times for the children to be alone as well as in small or large groups?

PLANNING THE PROGRAM:
7 ESSENTIAL PRINCIPLES AND ELEMENTS OF SCHOOL-AGE CARE

With the approach of summer, parents again face the recurring ritual of child care choices. This is what parents will be looking for in your summer and after-school programs.

Quality school-age care programs are tailored to the changing characteristics and needs of the children they serve. Professionals who operate the programs recognize these developmental changes and use them as positive opportunities to expand children's experiences.

1. Staff are resourceful, caring people who understand the important role that adults play in school-agers' lives.
2. Programs take into account that peer relationships are increasingly important to school-age children.
3. Programs use both mixed-age and same-age groupings for their activities.
4. Most activities and experiences are child-selected, rather than staff-selected. Schedules are flexible, and required participation in activities is limited.
5. Programs use positive guidance and discipline methods, rather than punishment, to help school-agers develop self-control and learn to behave appropriately.
6. Space is appealing and flexible. It can be used for different kinds of activities and different sizes of groups.
7. Programs provide a wide range of activities and experiences that contribute to all aspects of a school-ager's growth and development by:
    - fostering a positive self-image and a sense of independence.
    - encouraging children to think, reason, question and experiment.
    - enhancing children's physical development, encouraging cooperation, and promoting a healthy view of competition.
    - encouraging sound health, safety and nutritional practices and the creative wise use of leisure time.
    - generating an awareness of the community at large and creating opportunities for children's involvement in it.

(May, 1992)

(These seven principles were originally from a parent resource titled "Matching School-Age Child Care with Your Child's Needs" from Project Home Safe of the American Home Economics Association and are reprinted with permission.)

Summer? It's January! Right—the right time to begin planning for your summer program.

January -

Decide whether to have a summer program.
Decide the hours of care.
Decide how many children to serve, what ages, and how to group them.

February -

Decide central themes, slant, direction, goals and philosophy of program.
Use your summer folder.
Brainstorm with different levels:
- directors and the Board
- director and child care workers
- child care worker and children
- director and parents

March -

Advertise and pre-register participants.
- Send a newsletter or flier to present participants, past summer paticipants and your waiting list.
- Request a completed application and a deposit by a certain date.
Arrange for field trips.
- Decide major field trips that coincide with central themes.
- Make reservations for those that require them. (Competition can be fierce - especially for *free* field trips.)
- Working out transportation can often take months. Start early.
Write a grant, or exchange/combine resources with another program.
Arrange for specific classes - computer, gymnastics, swimming, horseback riding (Parents usually pay extra for opportunities such as these).

April -

Advertise for, interview and hire extra staff for summer.

Plan in-service training and orientation for staff.

Arrange for outside resource persons to participate in training in specific areas: developmentally appropriate practice, health and safety, conflict resolution, outdoor sports and games, arts and crafts.

May -

Plan specific activities on week-by-week basis related to central themes/goals/ideas.

Prepare Resource Packets for each week, containing:
- → background information on the theme
- → recommended resources for adult and books for the children
- → directions on how to do related activities
- → recipes
- → information on field trips

Send a letter to parents about:
- → starting and ending dates
- → details on policies, themes, field trips, lunch and snack, and rest
- → forms for medical information needed

Order supplies and resources.

Meet with staff from other programs or agencies who share the program space. For example, if you will be in a school site, meet with the school business manager and custodians to review policies and expectations. Try to anticipate potential problems before they occur.

1- 2 Weeks Before Summer Program Begins

Provide orientation and training for staff:
— Explain or review philosophy and goals
— Cover topics such as safety rules on playground, field trips, van or bus; growth and development specific to school-agers; effective discipline techniques; ways to ease children into the existing program, especially the shy and the overly aggressive child.

Make necessary changes in the physical environment.

Throughout the Summer

Every 2 weeks, meet as a group for 1-2 hours planning, evaluation and staff training.

2 Weeks After Summer Ends

Have an overall evaluation. This information will be used in planning for next summer.

Have each summer staff person begin a summer folder to be kept through the school year and used for planning for next summer. Into this folder will go: observations of special interests of individual children; crafts and other ideas suitable for summer. 捰

(This summer schedule first appeared in School-Age NOTES in March/April 1985 and was written by Bonnie Johnson in consultation with Jack Wallace of Nashville, Ellen Montanari of Phoenix, and Rudy Vanderburg of Oak Park IL.)

PLANNING THE PROGRAM:
READY FOR SUMMER?

In a phone interview Linda Sisson of the Edina Kids Club, Edina MN (currently Director of the National School-Age Care Alliance) and author of Kids Club: A School-Age Program Guide for Directors *shared her summer planning process.*

SAN: How early do you start planning for summer?

Sisson: We start the administrative planning in December and January. During the school year we serve over 600 children at 7 sites—the K-3 at their elementary school and the 4th-6th graders at one central site. During the summer we serve over 300 children but not all at one time. During administrative planning we will identify facilities for base sites since we have only three primary grade sites and the one site for the "Wise Guys Program" (older kids).

SAN: What is important in identifying those base sites?

Sisson: Our goal is to have not more than 50 children in one building. They need the feeling they are not in one large group all of the time.

Summer kids are what we call "lifers." Some spend seven years in our program. It is important to make summer different. Sites vary physically. The summer facilities should be set up with as much flexibility as possible. The environment should be comfortable and allow for an easy flow from inside to outside. Not all sites allow for this. School-agers need lots of room to be messy, lounge around, and have the feeling of privacy to be alone or have one-to-one time with their friends.

"You can't have a successful program that starts with piecemeal planning."

SAN: What else happens during this administrative planning period?

Sisson: We project enrollments and plan a budget. Staffing patterns are outlined and from our regular staff, positions are identified and we decide who will fill what slots.

SAN: What about programming and activity planning?

Sisson: We do our major planning such as setting central goals and major field trips.

In February we have a one-day retreat. We pair supervisors so they can work together in planning and do group activities or trips together. They take the central goals and our activity areas and start filling in their goal sheets. They start making charts and lists of activities, field trips, themes, special supplies, ideas for community service projects and money-making projects since that is such an important developmental need for the older kids.

SAN: So, is that it? It's all done?

Sisson: Heavens, no! From February through April we continue the planning, bringing the children into the process with their ideas and wants. In April we order supplies. During April and May we refine the activities and get specifics nailed down such as: daily routines; staff guidelines; put together a 2-day staff orientation; letter to parents; and children are assigned to groups.

SAN: What do you think is most important for directors to keep in mind as they plan their summer programs?

Sisson: I think there are three important concepts to keep in mind.

First, the pacing of summer is different from the before-and-after school program. During the school year many children are here only 10-15 hours a week. During the summer it's 45-50 hours a week. The pace slows down. There's time for getting completely absorbed in a project and following an idea all the way through.

Second, it is too easy to get caught up in the Field-Trip-A-Day summer plan. We learned the hard way that over time this leads to "field trip burnout." A field trip is a highly regimented activity. Field trips should be optional if some children find them boring and want less structure. Successful field trips are ones where the children are actively involved. There needs to be a balance of passive activities — riding a van, seeing a sight and riding the van back to the center — and active ones. An alternative to field trips might be putting on an art show in a local park pavilion. One of the things Jill Discher found the kids mentioned they liked more often than anything else was their homemade theme day. They might have a "formal day" when everyone gets dressed-up, they have a DJ to play music, and get to ride in a limo. Or they might have a flea market to raise money for a project.

Third, it's important to have central goals and see how the activities fit into the larger picture. You can't have a successful program that starts with piecemeal planning. We balance our program by defining activities that fit into five different play areas: Active Play, Constructive Play, Expressive Play, Mind Play, and Discovery Play. Each program needs to look at the different developmental needs of their children and plan from that point of view.

(February 1992)

PLANNING THE PROGRAM: SUMMER PROGRAMMING PLANNING

by Kathy Hermes

You already know how to involve kids in the day to day selection of activities, but this is your opportunity to give them a chance to fit into your summer program plans. This accomplishes two things: it gives them something to do now (thinking about the time out of school) and it also gives you the reassurance that the summer program will be what kids really want to do.

Here's how you can involve kids in your summer program planning.

First, pick a topic or theme that you think might be interesting.

Next, get a group of kids together who want to help plan. Working in a group, adults make suggestions of activities to get things going. As ideas are suggested, have a child write or draw the ideas being offered.

If the ideas come fast have more than one reporter. Include all ideas, even the silliest and most impossible. Look at the list and as a group decide what things would be the most fun to do with the time you will have available. It could be a day or a whole week. You may not agree with their wishes, but children need the chance to be wrong. You can then laugh together at your mistakes. Decide what their ideas would cost. Take the ideas that are not able to be used and put them in a dream box for another time. You might find that some of their ideas can be done before summer begins as part of your daily after-school program. Take the ideas from this brainstorming session and use them as you do your summer program planning.

Kids will be looking for fun, friendship and not too much pressure to succeed.

In most parts of the country summer means outdoor activities, so make sure to plan some activities that take advantage of the natural resources of your area. Whether you plan a variety of outdoor activities or take your entire group to day camp for a week, keep in mind that for children the outdoors is an exciting place.

An outdoor experience gives children the opportunity to gain self-reliance, have adventure and feel free in an outdoor setting. In today's world children don't often have that chance.

Different Expectations

Your activities should reflect the philosophy of your program. Parents will select a summer program for their child that provides the kind of experience they want. So if your material says you provide an academic enrichment like computers, be sure to include a good amount of it during the summer.

Parents will not be satisfied with the program if you do not deliver what they expected.

On the other hand, if your philosophy is to promote social development, a week at a nature camp could fit nicely into your plan.

Parents and kids usually make the choice of summer care together. Remember that they each expect different things from your program. Parents want safety, structure, and lots of activities. Kids, on the other hand, will be looking for fun, friendship and not too much pressure to succeed. They want to explore materials, relationships and achievement at their own pace.

For summertime outdoor programs that kids will enjoy, look at your community for ideas. You don't have to do all the planning. Contact a Camp Fire Boys and Girls Council or your Parks and Recreation Department to find out what opportunities are already being planned for school-age kids. Make sure you get information about costs, transportation and parent permission. Include the information in your registration material.

Whatever your plans are, have fun with it and capitalize on the benefits of those lazy summer days that we remember so well from our childhood.

(February 1992)

PLANNING THE PROGRAM: IDEAS FOR SUMMER PROGRAMMING

by Bonnie Cooper

Planning a summer program can be challenging and rewarding. Summer is a time when staff and children look forward to a change in their routines and environments. Some ideas for structuring long days and for planning special events are:

Structure the Day

Plan a daily schedule with time allotted for general types of activities. A sample schedule might include the following:

7:30 *Activities:* Children may become involved as they arrive.

9:00 *Small and Large Group Meetings/Snack:* Meetings are used to orient the children to the day and to develop camp spirit.

9:30 *Organized Games/Walking Trips:* Active games or activities are planned for a large group of children.

10:30 *Projects & Clubs/Visitors & Skill-Building Games:* Several on-going projects are planned for small groups of children: arts/crafts; dance; cooking; movement; music; nature; quiet games; drama; science

12:00 *Lunch/Quiet Choices*

1:00 *Nap/Games & Projects & Clubs/Special Event:* Younger children could nap. For older children, several activities can be planned or a special event offered for all children.

3:00 *Snack/Storytelling/Sing-Along/Free Choice:* Snack is served. Then children may listen to stories, be involved in a group sing-a-long, or have free choice time indoors, outdoors, or in the gym.

4:30 *Arts & Crafts/Make-it and Take-it/Organized Games*

5:30 *Children's Choice/Quiet Activities:* Children initiate ideas of their own choice.

Special Events

Plan occasions to bring children together for special activities. These events may relate to a theme for the day or week. Here are some ideas for special events:

Treasure Hunt: Create map or flag guides

Luau-Aloha Day: music, dancing, grass skirts

Circus/Carnival: Mini booths, prizes

Beach Party: Spread sand and beach towels

Fashion Show: Kids model their favorite outfits

Camping/Cookout: Set up tents, show camping gear

Wheels Day: Skates, bikes, big wheels-bike decorating, obstacle courses

Nature Scavenger Hunt: Find listed nature items

Halloween in July: Costume contest, bob for apples

Topsy-Turvy Day: Wear clothes backwards, etc.

Olympics: Games, relays

Water Works Day: Fire Dept. sprays kids

Balloon Day: Send-off, balloon stamp, decorating balloons

(Reprinted by permission from Child Care Newsletter for the Fairfax County Office for Children, Fairfax, VA)

(March/April 1986)

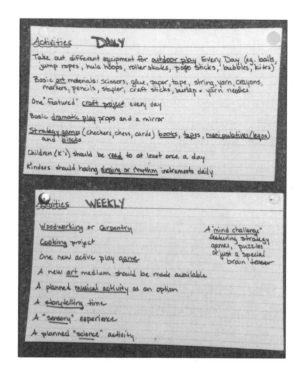

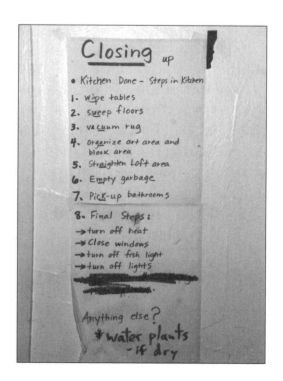

PLANNING THE PROGRAM:
HIRING AND TRAINING SUMMER STAFF

The following is adapted from an article by Rich Scofield in the March 1998 issue of Child Care Information Exchange *(CCIE) titled, "Staffing for Summer Programs."*

Hiring staff for school-age programs is always a challenge and it is no different for summer programs. It is a balance. While you look for staff who have the energy and enthusiasm to work with children and youth all day long, you must also find staff who have the maturity to be responsible for children particularly when out in the community and staff who may bring special skills and knowledge to the program.

Linda Eisele of After School, Inc. in Madison, WI recommends that staff be able to change and be flexible for a longer day. They need to be a more laid-back type of person. Often literally laid-back, they need to be comfortable laying on their backs just looking at the clouds with the children. High energy people are apt to burn out in full-day care. Summer programs need individuals who can pace and sustain themselves for the whole day.

It is important for staff "to be on the same page" — to understand the philosophy of the program and to be a team member. Getting staff "to be on the same page" requires careful screening in the hiring process and involving staff in the conceptualization and planning. Involving staff means they have an investment in how well the new staff do and in the success of the summer program.

One definition of "professional" is a person who can make on the spot decisions based on a body of specialized knowledge. "On-the-spot decision making" includes using common sense. But young staff often have not developed this yet. Letting the kids jump and roll around in the bushes on a trail hike may seem like fun for the kids but it isn't fun for the ecosystem and is not fun if it results in poison ivy. New staff might not recognize that letting kids sit on a railing with a 10 foot drop behind them is dangerous.

The job interview helps determine if applicants have common sense and can be flexible, adaptable, and creative. Ask "what if" and "how would you handle" questions. What would you do if you were in a gym with 10 children and one chair or one cardboard box? Obviously if they say line all the kids up against the wall and wait (as one interviewee did), the interview might as well be over.

Eisele suggests to determine how people think on their feet pose programming questions. "How would you structure a day?" "If it's raining what would you do?" "Here are some craft materials (or recycle materials), what could you do with them?" She says, "You want to find out if you toss out an idea, are they able to build on it and give you variations."

Joan Walker of the Percy Priest Extended Day Program in Nashville, TN likes to ask both in the interview and during training, "What are you most afraid of happening this summer?" — Answers vary: a medical emergency; losing or forgetting a child; the van breaking down; a child throwing up in the middle of a field trip. Joan throws these scenarios back to the staff to generate solutions. The discussion generated by these situations often produces ideas that Joan would not have thought of herself. Sharing such fears during training helps the staff bond.

Orientation must go beyond pass-in-the-hall training because summer staff often have no formal background in working with school-agers.

Tracey Ballas, past-president of the National School-Age Care Alliance, suggests putting two older school-agers on the interview team. When the kids ask a question, does the interviewee look at the children or look at the director. This might indicate how well they relate to and value children.

Always ask applicants about their skills, hobbies, special interests, and what they liked to do as children. These answers help both in selecting applicants and with ideas for programming that would involve the new staff person.

Orientation must go beyond pass-in-the-hall training because summer staff often have no formal background in working with school-agers. Ballas offers some advice on training. Remember new hires are most receptive in the first two weeks and it's hard to break bad or lax habits later. Use role plays and other active learning techniques since they may be visual, auditory, or kinesthetic/tactile learners. Your agenda may be policies and procedures. Their agenda is when do I get paid, where do I park, and how many breaks do I get. Answer their agendas first so they are comfortable and can listen to your agenda.

Summer with all the outdoor time and field trips is a time when there are more likely to be accidents, emergencies, or crises. Staff have to know the safety rules and procedures.

☞ Develop guidelines for the playground and for field trips.

☞ Post a chart of emergency treatment.

☞ Post emergency numbers by the phone and with the mobile phone.

☞ Put together a first aid kit.

☞ Post copy of treatment for insect bites and stings.

☞ Staff should know which children have allergies to not only insect stings but also poison ivy, peanuts, pets, and other animals.

☞ Always have staff on duty that are trained in CPR not just the director since summer days are eleven hours long and the director is not there all the time.

☞ Provide training and workshops for staff.

(May 1998)

PLANNING THE PROGRAM: PLANNING SUMMER: VOICES FROM THE FIELD

by Rich Scofield

January is a time that directors start looking at what their summer program might be like and begin some of their planning. This is a good time to hear from others on how they start their summer planning. *SAN* interviewed Joan Walker, director of the Percy Priest Extended Day Program in Nashville, TN for the past 10 years. She shared how her program views the overall planning and the planning of each day.

The Percy Priest program is parent-run and housed in an elementary school with its own dedicated space and access to other space in the school such as the gym and library. The school-year program has 84 children with a 1:12 adult-child ratio but the summer program has 30 children K-4th grade enrolled full-time with part-time/drop-ins bringing the per day total to 35-40. Five staff during the main part of the day means a 1:7-8 adult-child ratio. Field trips are 15-20 children, 3 staff and 1 van and 1 car. Two staff stay behind with the drop-ins. A "just-scrape-by" budget with 5 staff and 30 children is cushioned by income from the drop-ins. One program we spoke to had 120 children during the school year but scaled down to 60 in summer based on the number of children that would fit on a school bus.

What is a summer day?

One of the factors that needs to be accounted for in planning for summer is the difference in structure, time, and feeling of a summer day. It is a long day for both children and staff. Joan plans for three major "chunks" of time in the summer day: a 2-hour block in the morning before lunch, a 2-hour block in the early afternoon, and a block that is equivalent to a regular afternoon in the program which often can't use extended projects because of the varying pick-up times.

7a.m.-9:30 am: arrival time and program set-up (making sure all materials are ready and children have everything they need, particularly for field trips and swimming.) Children arrive often still sleepy and choose self-directed activities. Staff interact with the children but there are no planned adult-led activities.

9:30-11:30: snack, activity, project, guest speaker, field trip, or swimming

11:30-1:00: getting ready for and having lunch and rest time

1-3 pm: activity, project, guest speaker, or field trip

3-3:30: snack

3:30-6:00: activities and choices similar to regular afternoon during the school year

The planning of the large blocks of time includes not only the field trips but the themes and extended activities and long-term projects. It is all done before summer begins. Joan told us she finds it impossible to run the program and plan it at the same time.

Time for planning

Planning begins with Joan as director sitting down with the board of directors (her parents) and setting dates of operation, developing a budget, and setting fees. Setting dates is often compounded by the school district not announcing the summer closing and fall opening days of school far enough ahead.

Joan gives staff direction on planning such as finding groups of things to do around specific themes or activities e.g. cooking. During the spring she gives time to her staff to plan and gives them articles and books to get ideas. Staff use down times such as student study time (in a separate room) or daily prep time, one hour before children arrive, to gather ideas. Kids are queried about their ideas and suggestions often using a scrapbook from the previous summer to spark ideas.

Planning includes watching what fads, trends, movies, world events (Olympics, elections) the kids are interested in to develop themes. The hobbies and interests of staff and parents are also used as theme ideas. Thus, summer planning becomes an inclusive event involving all connected to the program which helps everyone become invested in its success.

(January, 1998)

(See page 29 for Joan Walker's planning time line for summer.)

PLANNING THE PROGRAM: PLANNING TIME LINE

The following summer program planning time line was developed by Joan Walker for use in her workshops on summer programming.

February

❏ establish dates of operation

❏ prepare budget based on projected enrollment and fees

❏ prepare registration forms and establish enrollment procedures

March

❏ begin registration of children

❏ brainstorm theme ideas with staff and children

❏ plan field trips which accompany themes

April

❏ make reservations for field trips

❏ arrange transportation, drivers, etc.

❏ assess staff availability

May

❏ provide in-service training to staff

❏ continue making field trip reservations

❏ outline weekly schedules and make daily lesson plans

❏ determine child groupings and pair with appropriate staff

❏ distribute program information to parents

❏ purchase as many supplies as possible in advance

June

❏ program begins - Smile and relax! You are prepared for a great summer!

August

❏ survey staff, children and parents to evaluate your program and generate ideas for next summer

September-January

❏ keep a file of ideas for summer by collecting newspaper and magazine articles, etc.

PLANNING THE PROGRAM:
LAST MINUTE CHECK LIST FOR SUMMER

❏ First-aid box is re-supplied.

❏ Develop traveling first-aid kit for trips, walks to the park, etc.

❏ Brief staff on emergency procedures including accidents and injuries, transportation breakdowns, lost children, late arrivals for trips, etc.

❏ Explain emergency procedures (e.g. fire drill) and day-to-day summer procedures.

❏ Update emergency phone number and medical information on children and staff.

❏ If sack lunches are necessary, let parents know what, when, and some appropriate items to include and those to keep at home (e.g. bottles, perishable foods).

❏ Prepare environment (rearrange old activity centers, develop new ones, gather rest time equipment).

❏ Double check staff schedules and children's day.

PLANNING THE PROGRAM: SUMMER PLANNING FOR LARGE PROGRAMS

The January 1998 issue of SAN had some examples of planning, scheduling, and registering from smaller summer programs (see page 27). The following involves larger, multiple programs.

Pamela Quinn, Recreation Supervisor for the Shaker Heights, OH Recreation Department and Treasurer for Ohio Professionals for School-Age Care, shared some of her approaches for summer programming.

She developed a non-traditional summer camp four years ago. They have between 400-500 children ages 2 1/2 thru 16 enrolled over a 9 week period in the summer.

They cut staff costs by using contractors for some of the activities as well as lowering material and supply costs. They begin planning the camp in October. The camp brochure is ready by January.

Regarding registration, Quinn says, "It is an enormous effort on our part to provide the fastest and easiest method of registration that we can. Every year, at the conclusion of camp, as a staff, we sit down and do a 'postmortem' so to speak on what went well and what didn't, how do we make registration more efficient and so on. Included in this meeting are clerical staff so everyone has input and we are all on the same page when it comes down to planning."

There are six summer camps run by the Recreation Department:

✺ **The Day School** at the Family Center is for 2 1/2 to 5 year-olds.

It includes half-day, 3/4 day, and full-day registration options. The enrichment and recreation activities are planned in three-week blocks that last year included water activities, multicultural festivals, and physical and large movement activities.

✺ **Rainbow Connection** is their traditional summer camp, offering a variety of activity choices. The K-3 program is at one site and grades 4-8 at another.

Parents and children fill out a "schedule worksheet" offering first and second choices during four daily activity sessions from 9:15-3:15 for each week. There are "schedule worksheets" for grades K-3, 4-5, and 6-8.

The K-3 have opportunities to sign up for over 30 activities including: crafts, ballet, soccer, gardening, games/puzzles/LEGO, hiking, and some extra fee and time activities like horseback riding. Grades 4-5 have additional options such as cartooning, archaeology, fast pitch skills, automobile design, volleyball and bowling (extra fee/time). Grades 6-8 have added activities such as wrestling, sculpture, and rock climbing (extra fee/time).

Before and after camp care is also provided for the Rainbow Connection attendees for a fee. Its description includes, "Activities will be structured so your child can relax after a day of excitement at camp or continue playing games and participating in sports or a special arts and crafts project."

☉ **C.I.T. Camp** ("counselor-in-training") is for ages 13-16.

This camp is an opportunity for middle and high school students to learn camp routines and develop leadership skills for future summer camp employment.

☉ **Camp Eagle** is for children with special needs where emphasis is placed on developmentally-appropriate recreational activities.

☉ **Specialty Camps** include Computer, Heritage, Nature & Science, Chess, Invention, and Summer Stock.

☉ **Sports Camps** consist of Basketball, Soccer, Fencing, Baseball, Lacrosse, Softball, and Tennis.

(March, 1998)

TIPS ON SUMMER PROGRAMMING

If most of your summer school-agers are also with you afternoons during the school year, then make the summer program as different from the rest of the year as possible. Since you may have the same kids each year, try to eliminate old and repetitive activities (unless requested by the children because they are favorites).

Day Camp Type Experiences

One technique for making summer different is to create a program similar to a day camp with camp-like activities.

1. Set up a tent on the playground (or set up a tent inside).
— A blanket or sheet over a stretched rope will do. Remember kids like small places to crawl into:
— It gives them the feeling of privacy if alone and the feeling of belonging (like a club) if with others.
— It gives them a feeling of less children in the room or that particular area. This contributes to a decrease in "territorial tension."

2. Create a badge program or activity classes.
— Use Scout books for ideas on this.

3. Kids and cooking
— Have the children think of the kinds of food they would have if they were camping. How can you provide similar experiences? (A hot dog and marshmallow roast over a charcoal grill?)

4. Swimming and water experiences
— If you can't arrange any swimming opportunities (local community pools often will let groups in before their regular hours), you can always resort to the hose or sprinkler. More innovative ideas are: water sliding on large plastic sheet anchored down over a grassy area, bathtub from salvage yard for outside water play (they can even climb in it!), go for a creek walk - look for crawdads, frogs, snails, minnows, etc.

5. Open-ended activities, experiences, and time upon which further exploration and interest can be built. (This includes time to be alone or time to just "do nothing.")

Examples -

Open-ended activities - cooking, reading, stitchery, woodworking, dramatic play using props such as old clothes, cardboard boxes and empty food cans and boxes.

Open-ended experiences

    Pets: Try some unusual pets, e.g. snakes, insects.

    Trips to parks: Make a list of all things that are: living, made of wood, made of metal, all things that are red, yellow, blue, etc.

    Invite people with specific skills to the program to talk about and demonstrate their skills - crafts people, artists, different occupations.

Open-ended time - Free time structured by a wide range of materials and equipment to explore and build with.

6. A quiet time or rest time (but not nap time) should also be planned.

The younger children (and sometimes older ones) will use it to sleep while the older children can read or play quiet games on the the floor. The Eakin Care Program in Nashville, TN uses this time for the children interested in keeping a summer diary to write the events of the day and their feelings about them. The younger children can draw a picture diary. Also, a summer reading contest can contribute to keeping "quiet time" quiet!

(May/June 1982)

MORE TIPS ON SUMMER PROGRAMMING

Grace Mitchell, the foremost specialist on day camp experiences offered the ideas on these two pages in her book Fundamentals of Day Camping *from 1961. Her advice still holds true today in planning for school-age experiences in summer programs. These excerpts from her book originally appeared in the May, 2000 and July 2000 issues of School-Age NOTES.*

On Choices:

Choice of Activity. The ability of a camper to choose his own program increases with age and experience. For the first week it is usually best to plan a program which exposes the camper to many activities. As the season progresses, more and more opportunity for choices should be offered. In some day camps the children have a planning period each day before they go home to discuss what they will do on the next day. In another, campers are given a choice of several activities with the leader keeping a check list to insure some degree of variety in each camper's program. The system used should allow for flexibility and for desirable changes.☻

On Where Kids Come From:

Background of Campers. The social, economic, and educational background of the campers will have some bearing on the program.

For the campers who live in crowded city areas where a tree is a novelty, the simplest outdoor experience may constitute high adventure.

On the other hand, many children who live in suburban homes with landscaped lawns and gardens, have just as great a need for open spaces in which to run, and for woods to explore. There are not many backyards today where the tree houses, huts, box and board building play, and junkyard type of equipment would be acceptable, but children have need of these things as an outlet for their energy and imagination. ☻

On Sensory Experiences:

The nature program can begin with the simplest sensory experiences. At no other season of the year can we live as intimately with nature as in the summer.

A camper can hear—

● wind in the trees and detect the difference between a broadleafed maple and a pine tree.

● water, lapping at the edge of a lake, dripping after a rain, gurgling and murmuring in a brook, or swirling down a drain.

● the sounds of insects…high and low pitch…rhythm, whirring, humming.

● the sounds of nature on a still hot day…on a windy day…on a rainy day…with his ear to the ground. ☻

On Balancing the Day:

Balance. A time for activity, and a time for rest; a time to be busy, and a time for leisure; a time to learn new skills, and a time to "just play;" this alternation is of utmost importance. Children with an overabundance of energy cannot be trusted to recognize their physical limits. Campers should go home at the end of the day pleasantly tired, but not physically exhausted. ✪

On Younger & Older Kids:

In camps where children under six are accepted, a program suitable for the preschool child is necessary. After they reach the age of ten, many campers acquire a sophistication which will call for a more challenging program than is satisfying to the younger campers. ✪

On Doing Nothing:

While he is looking at the program, the day camp director should bear in mind that it is not essential for every camper to be doing something all the time. The nicest gift we can give to some children is the opportunity to be still and do nothing; the finest thing we can teach them is to take time to STOP, LOOK, and LISTEN. Day camp can be an oasis in the midst of a world where pressure and haste prevail. ✪

On Rest Hour:

This may be called "siesta," or quiet hour. The terminology is not so important as the acceptance of the idea that campers and counselors need a time of inactivity in the middle of the day. The older campers may be more relaxed if they engage in quiet activity, such as knotcraft, sketching, or reading. The success of the rest hour will hinge on two factors: (1) the counselor must believe in it, and (2) the counselor must lie down with the campers. If he sits on a chair barking orders like a policeman such as, "Lie down," "Stop talking," "Who whistled?", he will supervise a wiggling, restless, resentful, and tense group of campers. If he stretches out on a blanket and says, "This really feels good. I'm tired after that long hike. Let's have a good rest, and then I will read some more of that story I started yesterday," his campers are more likely to follow his example.✪

PLANNING THE PROGRAM: LAST MINUTE IDEAS FOR SUMMER

by Rich Scofield

Most programs about now [June] are either just starting or just about to start their summer programs. The best intentions for having a well-planned summer program sometimes get pushed aside for the other 101 crises we in school-age care often find ourselves. Here are some last minute ideas to help.

Use Kids to Help Plan

Children and youth always respond better to their own ideas. Set up kid committees to help with this. This becomes an activity itself.

Bring the Community In

What professionals among your families could come in and explain what they do? Could you take a field trip to their work place?

Job Opportunities

Jobs can be wonderful experiences for school-agers. Start with application and interviews. Use schedules and time cards. Provide compensaton, if not money then rewards such as extra time at the park or pool, or front seat in the van for long field trips. Ideas for jobs: cooking, cleaning, office chores, answering the program's phone, yardwork, putting away supplies, caring for a younger child.

Use Scavenger Hunts to Keep Museum Trips Interesting

The March issue reported on the sumer program for older kids in Baltimore, MD that found museum and educational trips were not the greatest successes of various trips planned.

When discussing such issues in Hastings, NE, one SAC program explained that incorporating a scavenger hunt into the museum field trip was enough to keep children interested. For the scavenger hunt the kids had to find which exhibits had the items mentioned on the scavenger list. Maybe for your program the first trip to a museum could be one in which the kids could decide which items should be included in a scavenger hunt.

In Allentown, PA one of the seminar participants mentioned that museums often make up their own scavenger hunts that they give out to groups.

So next time you plan a trip to a museum call ahead to see if they have scavenger hunt lists.

Inexpensive Resources

The Cub Scout and Girl Scout books are inexpensive and have tons of ideas especially ones for summer. Plus, the Girl Scout badge system is a ready made set of themes for you.

Theme Ideas

Wedding themes seem to be popular in several parts of the country. Programs report that the boys actually enjoy participating contrary to stereotypical views.

A real estate theme was used by one program in Pennsylvania. The kids decided on the type of house to buy, talked with a real estate agent, went through the real estate ads, learned about how much money a family would have to earn to afford the house, and the kids were really excited when by coincidence on a field trip they drove by the house they had selected.

Unique Activity Idea

A program in Oregon goes treasure hunting by buying small polished stones by the pound at rock shows and then putting them in the sand pile or dirt pile to be "found." The beauty of it is that the kids keep finding the "gems" for months and even the next summer.

Easy Planning for Next Year

All summer take photos and videos of trips and activities plus save crafts, art work and any daily journals and kid newsletters. Next spring each week put a couple of photos, crafts, etc. out to spark the children's ideas about what they want to do and where they want to go and before you know it your planning for summer is off and running.

(June, 1993)

PLANNING THE PROGRAM:
LONG RANGE PLANNING

The following are some approaches to summer programming. All involve long range planning. Many programs incorporate a blend of all three approaches.

Field Trips

For programs with transportation, this approach keeps them going as much as possible, taking advantage of warm weather and availability of recreational/educational facilities.

Get on the phone [in March and April] to locate places to go and happenings in your community. Always ask if they know of any other places in town for children to visit. For new programs or people unfamiliar with what's available for children to visit, call Scout organizations, other centers and local principals for ideas.

Badge System

Most programs don't have readily available access to transportation or have to share it with pre-school, church, senior citizens, etc. These programs need something to keep the children motivated and interested. The Jane Addams Center, Chicago, and the Teaching Centers, Wauwatosa, WI use a badge system similar to Scouting.

A badge system can work in many different ways. It helps children to set short term and long term goals. There can be several levels to each badge (beginners, intermediate, expert) just as Red Cross has several levels to each class of swimming. These various levels help to deal with the wide age range, level of ability and varying degree of interest that are in each program.

Workshops, classes, activity periods — whatever you want to call them — planned activity times can help the children complete the tasks required for each badge. This is where real planning skills are needed.

1. *Plan the kinds of badges* that one can earn around the types of activities you usually have in the summer plus the expertise and interests of your staff. These badges may be swimming, cooking, sewing, woodworking, collecting, animal lore, city lore, bookworm, penpal, etc. Use Scout books for further ideas and to help create your own ideas for badges.

2. *Plan the list of activities to earn each badge*. Break the badge activities into levels. For example, one requirement of the beginner Bookworm Badge may be to read or have a teacher read to them one book. For the intermediate or expert levels more books may be required.

3. *Plan the activities that will help the children earn their badges*. If making a book or scrapbook is a requirement of the Bookworm Badge, then activity time, materials and instruction for that opportunity will have to be planned for each week.

An advantage of this approach is that once you've planned the badges and requirements for each level, you have built a framework into which you plug your daily/weekly plannings and activities. A side benefit of the badge system can be parent involvement by allowing children to work on badges at home.

Interdependent Activities In a Coordinated Program

This is the most challenging approach to plan and implement as summer programming. It requires a set of long range plans that can be flexible and responsive to spontaneous events and immediate needs. The interdependent and coordinated parts refer to the concept of making activities and events relate to each other and to general program goals and aims. Some programs may call this a *theme approach*.

Summer camps often use Indian culture and lore as a basis of their activities. The Teaching Centers (Wauwatosa, WI) use a theme approach the entire year. One year the theme was *Heritage, USA*. Activities centered around different ethnic backgrounds and cultures. Think of all the activities one could plan around cultures using food, dances, songs, books, films, trips, crafts, etc. Another year was planned around *Science in Your Backyard*, including Animal Life, Plant Life, Astronomy and Space Travel.

When planning take into consideration the children's needs. How can you incorporate block play, dramatic play, their penchant for making lists and collecting things, their desire for "real tools, real work" — such as cooking— and the older children's concerns related to money earning projects? Finally, make sure that spontaneous events and needs of each child are not overlooked because of concern with the theme. The child who has a parent or sibling in the hospital may provide an opportunity for others to learn about caring, such as making and sending Get Well cards. This also may give the child some attention that he/she is suddenly without because of the crisis at home. It may bring up other children's concerns, interests, and fears around doctors, hospitals and getting sick, which may all come out through lots of doctor-hospital play. While one might stretch a theme to cover such unplanned life events — Indian medicines and medicine man costumes, various cultural home remedies, growing medicinal plants in your backyard — one must remember that the children's needs and interest are the real basis of the program.

NOTE: INVOLVE THE CHILDREN IN THE PLANNING

Their investment and interest in any project is important to the project's success. Ask for their ideas, opinions, concerns involving themes, trips, activities. They initially may need adult-contributed choices and ideas to spark their own creativity.

Problems and Considerations

Transportation - This is a stumbling block for many programs. Generally retail leasing/rental rates (from rental agencies and car dealers) are out of most budget ranges. However, figure out ways of emphasizing advantages to them for donating or leasing at discount — such as tax deductions, community service, publicity. If any board members are with large companies that buy or lease vans, this might give you an edge.

Check the following:
- — Churches with buses not being used during the week.
- — Social service and private clubs/associations that don't use their vans regularly.
- — Social service agencies that use vans may be interested in renting a van at an affordable rate to bring in a little extra income for the agency.

Grouping - Most after-school programs find grouping necessary for summer programming. Typical grouping is by age with names for each group (children can choose their own names). Also, the groups are assigned a primary caregiver (group leader). A consideration in grouping and assigning kids to group leaders is to match up: a) early morning kids with early staff person, b) late afternoon kids with late (close-up) staff person.

One other consideration in grouping children and assigning primary caregivers is the difference in personalities.

(March/April 1981)

PROGRAMMING CONSIDERATIONS:
CHANGING FOR SUMMER

If this summer you have the same children, same adults, same environment, and same program, you should consider how to change and rearrange these to provide an exciting and challenging summer program.

Change the Environment

Rearrange the rooms you use. Make them very different for summer. Have the children help plan the rearranging. Add or subtract tables, furniture, shelving, lighting, wall decorations. Add lots of soft space for the slower pace of summer — overstuffed chairs, carpeting, floor pillow. Add new interest centers and put away old interest centers. Add tent type structures to both indoor and outdoor spaces. Add to playground new building materials such as old tires, boards, barrels (paint them bright colors to avoid junkyard look), and make sure water play is available. Move some of the interest centers outside for the day, such as art easels and woodworking. Plan lots of field trips, even it if only means walking to a nearby park.

Change the Children

Rearrange groups. Perhaps break into age groupings and assign primary caregivers. Allow friends to visit. Arrange for some children to visit another center and vice versa.

Change the Adults

Arrange for guest instruction by adults (including parents and teen-age siblings) who have special talents and skills. Check with public relations departments of police, fire departments, hospitals, armed services recruitment offices, manufacturers; many have school visit programs designed for elementary-aged children and they are not as busy in the summer. Just as you might have some children switch centers for the day, have an adult or two from the other center switch places (visit) for the day.

Change the Program

Changing the environment such as different interest centers and more field trips is part of programming differently. New interest areas might include new pets, cooking or snack preparation (more time for this is available during the summer). Visit where parents work. Try different themes or units. Arrange with a computer store to sponsor a computer camp at your center. Borrow video tape equipment and have kids film their own movie.

Brainstorm with others (and with the children) to find ways of changing the above four elements of your program to create a summer that all enjoy.

(May/June 1983)

PROGRAMMING CONSIDERATIONS: SUMMER PROGRAM TIPS

Try some new ideas for your summer program. Children and teachers need the stimulation of something different as well as the change of pace summer provides. Looking for new ideas and different approaches can often give summer programs the shot in the arm they need. This summer take your good ideas and put them into action.

Have Your Tried This?

Have a contest to name the summer program (The Summer Seekers, Kid's Alive, Summer of Friends, Exploring Unlimited, Adventure Time Program, Summer Raiders).

How about a Mascot? An Emblem? (Kids can draw them) Relate them to a summer program name or theme.

A Program Theme Song? A Password? Secret Handshake?

Have a panel of children selected by the other children be the judges for choosing the above or have a lesson in democracy by taking a vote.

New Kids

Often in the summer program there is a sudden influx of new children.
- Make sure they get paired up with someone who can help them learn your program's routine.
- Give them two rules to guide their behavior (these can apply to others as well):
    1. We don't do anything that might hurt ourselves or others.
    2. We don't do anything that might destroy property.
- Do a bulletin board featuring the new kids — pictures of their family, pets, friends, drawings, special interests.
- At the end of the first week, send home a note to the child's family about how well the child has adjusted.

(May/June 1983)

PROGRAMMING CONSIDERATIONS: "LIFERS" IN SAC: SUMMER PROGRAM CHALLENGE

Linda Sisson of Kids Club in Edina, Minn. (currently Executive Director of the National School-Age Care Alliance) has referred to those school-agers who start in kindergarten and stay with the program for 6-7 years as "lifers." (In child care programs that start at birth, the number of years in the same program could conceivably be 9, 10, or 11 years.) Those children go through many, many staff changes and often out last directors.

New staff and new directors need to be aware of this issue when planning both the after-school program and the summer program. The existence of "lifers," long-term attendees, underscores the importance of not having a program based on continuous activities with no sense of purpose. It also emphasizes the importance of involving the kids in the planning. Continuous activities and programming without consideration of developmental and individual needs leads to burnout by both kids and staff.

Many of the older children have been at the same facility since they were preschool age. It is difficult to provide that much challenge and variation of experience in a single facility over a long period of time.

The following passage about "lifers" comes from *School's Out! Group Day Care for the School Age Child* (1974) by Elizabeth Prescott and Cynthia Milich. Though more than 20 years old, this passage is still relevant:

"The problems most often described (at 40% of the centers) for summer programs is that of keeping children busy, most especially older boys. Many of the older children have been at the same facility since they were preschool age. It is difficult to provide that much challenge and variation of experience in a single facility over a long period of time.

"Boys, especially, seem to hanker for more challenge and variety. They would welcome chances to get out into the community, to explore on bicycles, and poke around and perhaps build tree houses or forts with friends. It is this very kind of activity which is most difficult for group care to provide. The long summer day is often too hot for the organized sports which hold interests during the school year. What to do clearly is a problem for the staff."

What to do?

School-Age NOTES over the years has discussed different ways of addressing the issue of making the summer program interesting, relevant and different to children who have been attending for many years rather than focusing on keeping them busy.

- ❂ **Plan for some activities and experiences to occur in a totally different setting** - local church, camp site, community parks, library, or computer center.
- ❂ **Plan for overnight events** even if it is only a "lock-in" at your program. Have a campfire on the playground, roast marshmallows and other traditional summer camp evening activities.
- ❂ **Utilize local libraries, Cooperative Extension and 4-H offices, Girl Scout and Boy Scout books and other community resources** that have information on camping, water sports and activities, arts & crafts projects, games, songs, and anything else that will make your program special.

(June 1994)

PROGRAMMING CONSIDERATIONS: THE NOISE FACTOR — A PLACE FOR EVERYTHING

by Rich Scofield

We should provide "a place" to be noisy.

How do we deal with the conflicting issues of the negative effects of noise and the need of children to let go and make noise? (Or we could ask: Does noise have a place in our programs?) Summer time, with more accessibility to outdoor play, may provide a solution to the old adage "A place for everything and everything in its place."

School-age care professionals know first hand about school-agers' need to let out pent-up energy after sitting in quiet classrooms all day or even just being indoors. Mary Rivkin, in her NAEYC book *The Great Outdoors*, says "Being outdoors can provide a fine sense of freedom. …One's body is no longer under need of tight control—its capabilities to shout, sing, leap, roll, stretch, and fling are unleashed. Outdoor voices are suddenly acceptable."

So, we should provide "a place" to be noisy. That this "place" should be outdoors rather than inside gained more credence with research results announced in May, 1997 about the effects of noise and reading skills.

Noise and reading ability are linked – children who live in noisy areas have poorer reading skills than those in quieter areas. Now, the first study to explain that link suggests that it is because children in noisy areas find it harder to recognize and understand human speech. *New Scientist* news service reports that researchers at Cornell University found that 7- and 8-year-old children from a school that lies in the flight path of one of New York City's airports had poorer reading skills than same-age children from a quiet neighborhood. The researchers also found that those children from flight-path neighborhoods found it harder to recognize and understand spoken words. The researchers concluded that in order to cope with the din, the children near the airport cut down the burden of noise they were exposed to by "filtering out" certain sounds, including human speech.

Maybe this will be a wake-up call as to the importance of lowering group sizes, particularly in "acoustically-challenged" cafeterias and gyms. In an article on dedicated space in the November 1993 issue of *SAN*, this author makes the following observations.

"They almost seem as if they were made to create noise. In a sense, cafeterias and gyms with high ceilings, smooth floors, and unadorned walls are perfect for bouncing sounds.

"I have walked into a cafeteria in which each child was appropriately engaged. Children were at tables participating in activities, playing board games and the older kids were sitting on a rug socializing. None of the behavior individually was too noisy, inappropriate, or out-of-control and yet the din pulsated in my ears. It was too loud.

"We know that noise can be a stress factor in the workplace. One can only wonder at the stress for a child in a noisy gym or cafeteria for 2-3 hours a day all week long. And what about the stress on the caregiver who has inside duty all of the time? No one has looked at the issue of noise as a stress factor in school-age care."

With our summer programs being all day, it is even more important for staff to look at noise issues and provide places such as the outdoors where children and youth can let their exuberance follow its natural course.

(June 1997)

PROGRAMMING CONSIDERATIONS:
WHERE EVERYBODY KNOWS YOUR NAME

"Sometimes you want to go, Where everyone knows your name, And they're always glad you came…" The theme song for the famous TV show, *Cheers*, is poignant and longing. It conjures up images of ourselves as alone and unknown. Both our basic fear and need are touched. We long for and treasure places where we are recognized and accepted, where people know our name.

These needs are probably related to instinctual survival: recognition by our mother who will provide sustenance AND belonging to a group which will furnish security and protection from outside dangers. Whatever the reasons behind our need to be known, we do know that the need is strong.

In June, an influx of new children will enter school-age programs as they start their all-day summer schedule. These kids will be faced with getting acquainted with a new environment, with new peers, with new adults. They will look for ways to make themselves known. They will gravitate to spaces that feel secure and to people who greet them with gladness.

We can help children accomplish these goals by planning experiences, for the first month, where they can:

● Make name tags and labels out of a variety of materials: paper and crayons, burned into wooden name plates, string and glue on cardboard; glitter and glue on cloth; acrylic paint on tee-shirts; cloth hats; headbands; and alphabet beads on string.

● Draw "family trees;" look up the meaning of names; tell stories of "how I got my name;" make lists of relatives and famous people with the same name.

● Label works of art, themselves, their individual space, and their "This is me" projects.

(May/June 1989)

PROGRAMMING CONSIDERATIONS:
SUMMER FIRST AID FOR PARENTS

by Kate Hacker

Many details and a staggering variety of tasks to consider are involved in planning a summer school-age program. Consideration of parents might not seem a high priority in the midst of all this planning flurry. However, the quality of the program will be enhanced by a conscious consideration of the needs of busy parents in the summer.

The first contact with many parents will be when they inquire about the program with a view to enrolling their child. This is an important contact for the center and for the parent because it can create a lasting first impression. Arrange for a staff member who has been a part of the planning team and has good rapport with parents to handle these initial contacts. In this initial interview the staff person can assure the parent that:

1. their child will be safe and well cared for;
2. the center has planned a program of such diversity that the child will have fun;
3. the parent will always be aware of the schedule of activities and trips;
4. the parent is encouraged to take time off and join in the fun.

Many situations in a summer program can give parents anxiety about their children's safety. The center staff is responsible for assuring parents that safety is a priority of the program and its staff. Some of these concerns will be allayed by posting and including in the summer brochure all of the center's safety measures, policies and procedures. Up-to-date emergency numbers are especially important in the summer because of the centers' increased activity schedule and traveling on field trips. Encourage parents to provide extra emergency numbers because of vacation schedules.

Designate at least one staff person to greet kindergarteners and their parents when they arrive. These parents need special attention in the summer. Kindergarteners are coming from a "protected" preschool environment and many parents are anxious about the contact with the "older" children. Some are afraid their little ones will get lost or bullied unmercifully. Reassure parents that their children will be closely watched and will have a scheduled nap or rest time every day.

The center's summer brochure can convey a spirit of fun and excitement, can

give details of the activities and welcome them to participate in their child's summer day. A catchy name that is different from the one used during the year helps capture the spirit of summer and, if the brochure is printed on bright, summer colored paper, it catches the eye and attention. One help for parents is to make a "month-at-a-glance" list of field trips and special theme days on a tear-off sheet to be posted in a conspicuous place in the home. Field trip permission slips can also be attached to the brochure, have one for each field trip. This method encourages the parents to remember the field trip date because there is a deadline for the permission slip.

These organizational details can avert misunderstandings and will convey to the parents that their children are in good hands. The intangible and essential first aid for parents in the summer is a sensitive staff who has an understanding and empathy for the challenges of working parents. A welcoming smile from the staff and a happily tired child is very soothing medicine for parents at the end of the day.

(May/June 1991)

EVALUATING SUMMER SKILLS

The issue of measuring outcomes and evaluting the effectiveness of school-age programs has come to the forefront particularly in light of the push for enrichment/ academic programs. What may get overlooked are the non-academic skills learned after school and in the summer. The following list can easily be expanded to areas such as socialization, communication, or particular areas of focus such as music. The list could also be used as a pre-test, post-test measure of how your summer program affects each child, and then use positive results as a marketing tool to let parents and the community know what children "learn" in your program.

This list was originally developed by the McNeilly Day Home, one of the original "settlement houses" in Nashville, and now named the McNeilly Center for Children. The following is the introduction to the article originally titled "Skills and Kids" appearing in our May/June 1987 issue of SAN:

Wondering if you are providing developmentally appropriate activities? Or, have you been concerned about a particular child's skills? Use the checklist [on page 51] to evaluate both individual skills and the availability of skill-building activities in your program. [Include] a section on water skills if swimming is a large part of your summer program.

Fine Motor Activities

Arts

____Painting

____Cutting and gluing

____Collage Making

____Box Sculpture

____Sand Casting

____Drawing

____Rubbings

____Printing

____Clay

Others

____Billiards

____Ping Pong

Sewing, weaving, & knitting

____Dye cloth or yarn; tie-dyeing

____Knit a variety of items: scarves, doll sweaters, ties, belts, arm bands and head bands

____Embroidery stitches

____Pot holders - weaving

____Burlap wall hangers

____Macrame - plant hangers

____God's eyes

____Hand puppets

____Sew curtains, purses, laundry bags, pillows

____Sew and stuff sit-upons

____Patchwork quilts

____Crochet

Building & Construction

____Putting together a variety of types of materials to make a product: Kazoos, insect cages, models

____Building with scrap wood: hammering, sawing, drilling

____Designing & building a project

____Repairing a piece of equipment: fence, benches, sandboxes

____Lego materials

____Unit Blocks

____Popsicle sticks

____Tinker toys

____Erector sets

____Soap box cars

Gross Motor Activities

____Jumps rope with ease

____Runs gracefully

____Roller skates (or roller blades)

____Skips with a consistent flow

____Throws a small 4" ball with ease

____Catches a small ball with some skill

____Throws a medium 8" ball with ease

____Catches medium ball with some skill

____Can "bat" to some degree

____Can hop-scotch with some skill

____Has some tumbling skills

____Wrestles on a one to one basis

____Has a good sense of rhythm

____Enjoys dancing and movement to music

____Kicks an 8" ball with some accuracy

Team Sports

____Hockey

____Soccer

____Relay Games

____Baseball

____Football

____Basketball

____Kickball

Developing Real-Life Skills

____Collating and other office work

____Setting tables for lunch

____Cleaning up the grounds and building

____Cooking

____Sewing to make a profit

____Fundraising projects: bake sales, plant sales, craft sales

____Planting a garden

____Assisting with younger children

____Planning special activities with staff

Group Activities

____Playing School

____Going on field trips

____Dramatic play

____Hide-and-go-seek

____Organized clubs of other sports

____Playing table games: Monopoly, Checkers, Concentration, Battleship, Card Games, Jacks

MARKETING:
PLAN FOR SUMMER NOW—REAP MARKETING REWARDS LATER

by Rich Scofield

Each year by January 31st Rick Porter knows what field trips and choices of activities the children in his nine programs will have available to them each day in summer. He will be able to describe in his summer brochure exactly what the children will be doing and what the themes will be week to week. This not only helps the program run smoothly but by having the availability of choices mapped out, the detailed programming plans act as a marketing tool attracting parents who want a variety of activities and experiences for their children.

Porter says, "Even more important than a marketing tool in a brochure is the reassurance when summer comes that the program actually does the activities it said it would do." By the time their children are school-agers parents are likely to have experienced programs that sounded good in terms of global generalizations in slick brochures, but the kids went to the same parks for field trips and choices of activities were limited and repetitious.

Rick Porter has been running after school and summer programs since the 1980's. He is the Executive Director of Rainbow River/Rainbow Rising School-Age Programs of Hermosa Beach, Calif. near Los Angeles.

Three of Porter's nine programs are for-profit and six are non-profit. They have three large school buses and three large vans. It is obvious that coordinating field trips among nine programs is a big job. Porter explained that the school-agers are away from their centers three days a week. One day they are at a park or local pool, another day they go to the beach, and the third day is a regular field trip such as to a bowling alley or a special destination like Knott's Berry Farm.

All the program plans and information are kept in a large three-ring binder for each site. One of the advantages is that staff who may not have the experience and skills to plan each day can see exactly what choices to plan for. Porter likes to have three or four planned activities for both indoors and outdoors each day. The other advantage is that staff can see what supplies they will need to have ready.

Included in the advance summer planning are two big overnight camp outs. One of them has 300 kids and is set in an urban park.

Porter's experience sets a good example for the wisdom in planning summer programs far in advance.

Do you have your summer plans ready?

(February 2000)

MARKETING SUMMER PROGRAMS

"Summer programs for a child care center can be a marketing, management and programming challenge." This understatement is the opening sentence of the chapter on summer programs in Nan Lee Howkins' book *Profitable Child Care: How to Start & Run a Successful Business*.

✔ **Analyze what you can offer that gives your program an edge in a competitive market.** Howkins advocates this as an approach to planning summer. Whether you are for-profit or non-profit, your program is affected by many of the same forces. She points out that often centers experience enrollment drops in summer "with a consequent decrease in income." "Marketing becomes crucial as the competition from many other sources increases."

✔ **Know your competition and "pinpoint their weaknesses."** Howkins realizes, "The first factor that parents look at will be price." She believes there are many lower priced care situations. This could be because of informal programs such as care by a teenager or family day home or drop-in programs such as Boys and Girls Clubs or city recreation departments. Can you provide better adult:child ratios, a safer environment, or more unique programming opportunities? These advantages are what you want to point out and highlight in your marketing efforts.

✔ **What you plan to include in your summer program can become a marketing tool.** According to Howkins, "You can gain an advantage over your competition with a special program or extra-exciting field trips and activities for the children….The purpose of designing and publicizing each special feature is to convince parents that your program offers something to their child that is worth the extra cost over other summertime activities." These strategies can work for both for-profit and non-profit programs.

✔ **Do you make your fees all inclusive or charge extra?** What we hear from other programs across the country is a mixture. Some programs publicize special activities such as dance or gymnastics that are available for extra fees and contracted with by outside instructors who come to the program site. Some programs build the expense of these opportunities into their fee structure so it introduces all children to the experience. They use either outside instructors, volunteers, or staff with the needed expertise.

✔ **Continually educate parents as to the benefits their children receive in your program.** Howkins stresses that you can emphasize the advantages of your program "without directly criticizing another program." Remind parents of your safety procedures, quality standards adhered to, qualifications of staff, and access to special opportunities. These can be put in a brochure or flier to educate your own parents. Howkins gives the following as examples:

Did You Know:
- That our fine staff ratios stay the same during summer?
- That there will be special activities for each age group…even on rainy days?
- That, even in the summertime, our staff will meet our strict training requirements, including knowledge of first aid?
- That all our staff are 18 or older?
- AND FINALLY, that the space is LIMITED so that there isn't over crowding? [Howkins p. 137]

(Nan Howkins' *Profitable Child Care: How to Start & Run a Successful Business* (1993) 270 pages is available in hardback from: Facts on File, Inc., 460 Park Avenue South, New York, NY 10016 800-322-8755.)   *(March 1999)*

MARKETING:
HAVE A SUMMER SAFARI:
START NOW RECRUITING ENROLLMENTS FOR SUMMER

Get parents and kids excited about your summer program early by having a "Summer Safari" Day. Every director knows that early recruitment for the summer program is a must for optimum planning. When folks are in the midst of winter doldrums, give them something to look forward to by providing a summer day.

- **Set up the program area with summer type games and activities** that give the children and their parents a taste of what the summer has in store for them. Be sure everyone gets a name tag so friendships can begin forming.

- **For every registered child give a summer program T-shirt** with the program logo or other design. Or maybe offer refrigerator magnets or some other giveaway that will help families stay excited about the program.

- **Going to sing lots of songs** during the summer? Have songbooks ready and someone to lead the children in a few songs.

- **If you've already hired your summer staff, introduce them** to the children and parents. Display posters with the planned field trips.

- **Have summer-type refreshments on hand.**

- **While the parents are completing registration forms, take a Polaroid picture of each child wearing a safari hat or pith helmet,** perhaps standing in front of a mural of a jungle scene.

The excitement generated from this special event will guarantee enrollments!
(*This idea is from* 250 Management Success Stories, *published by* Exchange Press, P.O. Box 3249, Redmond WA 98073-3249, 800-221-2864, www.ccie.com)

(January, 1997)

MODEL PROGRAMS: ZOO CAMPERS ENCOUNTER "THE INTERRELATIONSHIP OF ALL LIVING THINGS"

by Dale Fink

For those in the school-age field who want to offer a program during the summer that is completely different from what goes on during the school year, the council for Greater Boston Camp Fire Boys and Girls has hit on a winning formula. "At first," Executive Director Cynthia Beaudoin acknowledges, "we were just going to run a regular camp program on the zoo grounds – making one hour excursions into the zoo itself, the way any other day care or camp group might come in from the outside." But what evolved was a much more compelling program model. Their "Zoo Camp" wasn't merely located at the zoo; rather it was an integrated experience, with games, arts, crafts, and social interaction organized around the study of zoo animals and their habitats.

The notion of even running a camp for 60 to 100 school-agers per week on the grounds of the zoo may seem implausible to some.

The notion of even running a camp for 60 to 100 school-agers per week on the grounds of the zoo may seem implausible to some. But once Beaudoin and her Council discovered "the Sausage," an elongated, untended piece of land which "was empty, wild and weedy," they just knew they had to have it for their kids! For years the Council had been busing city children 20 miles to a suburban summer day camp (and they still do). But here was a large piece of open green space located in the heart of urban Boston, bordering predominantly African-American neighborhoods and completely safe and secure because it lay within the perimeters of the zoo's fencing. And not a soul was using it for anything. "An underutilized space for an under-serviced population," as Beaudoin put it.

A $15,000 grant from the Bank of Boston gave them enough to move forward with an aggressive plan. Permits had to be obtained from city officials. Electricity, a telephone and water had to be extended to "the Sausage." Port-a-potties had to be brought to the site. A set of temporary steps had to be installed. For an "office and a place to lock up materials, a trailer of the kind used on construction sites was leased for them by a corporate donor – but it had to be dropped onto "the Sausage" from outside a high fence by a "cherry picker," also donated. The Metroparks Franklin Park Zoo staff agreed to leave up an outdoor tent they had erected for an unrelated purpose as the "indoor" space on very rainy days. On days that were just moderately rainy, "we all went around with our umbrellas and ponchos."

Once they knew they could make the site workable, they needed a program plan. That is when they discovered how well the philosophy of Camp Fire and that of Metroparks Zoo meshed: both declared in virtually the same language in their educational materials that they wanted children to "understand the interrelationships of all living things." One of the Franklin Park Zoo's education staff turned out to be available for the summer; she was hired by Camp Fire as their "Zoo Resource Person." With her intimate knowledge of the zoo and its staff, the program began to fly.

The camp's weekly themes were organized around what they called 'FFESS Time" (Furs, Feathers, Ecoskeletons, Skins, and Scales). Each group of eight children had one counselor and one junior counselor, and they gave themselves FFESS related names when they formed at the start of each week: for instance, the "African Mud Turtles." There were three large group gather times per day, which were called "Harambee" rather than "Council Fires," with a nod to the African focus of the zoo and the African genealogical roots of the majority of the campers.

Kids handled an 11-foot Burmese python (which eats small cattle). They studied the South American trumpeter bird. They became familiar with the small creatures brought around by the "Wild on Wheels" zoomobile. They were allowed to go in and out of the zoo's educational resource rooms whenever there were no other programs already scheduled there. They made papier mache masks of animals. The game "statue" was renamed "Possum." They ended each week with skits, songs, and role play about the animals they had studied.

The weekly parent fee was $60, with 75% of the children subsidized by "camperships," including some purchased by Digital for its own employees' children. Every participating child received a junior membership in the zoo for $10, paid by the family, good for free admission for one entire year.

Zoo Camp drew an unexpectedly large number of children age ten and older – both girls and boys. Beaudoin commented that the discipline problems were minimal, as children became really engaged in the experience, under the guidance of an enthusiastic staff, which was racially and sexually balanced. Assuming they can retain the support they received from their corporations and foundations, both the zoo and Camp Fire are looking forward to continuing the experiment for at least three years.

(January/February 1991)

MODEL PROGRAMS:
KIDS ON WHEELS:
A UNIQUE SUMMER PROGRAM

Kids On Wheels is a unique summer program developed out of necessity by the Niños Group, Inc., a for-profit child care company in San Antonio, Texas. It was initiated in 1986 to fill the school-age summer care needs of employees at a hospital where the Niños Group ran a preschool child care center.

Not having a van, gym or swimming pool for a summer program meant developing creative alternatives. The program was designed around the city bus system.

How It Works

At the beginning of the summer the children take a field trip to the central bus terminal to learn how the system works. Then they pin the bus system map to a wall at the center and plan their trips by where they can go by bus. To do that the children select 12 themes to explore during the summer program. They use the yellow pages to find addresses that are on bus routes.

Where They Go

The kids spend the summer "on wheels" learning about local historical sites, architecture, tourist attractions, the airport and photography.

What They Do

The children make a scrapbook of their trips, using photographs, tape recordings, and interviews. They also design and make a group tee shirt that they wear on all field trips. The weekly schedule is: on Mondays, they plan the trip; Tuesday through Thursday they go on field trips learning about the city and also go swimming on those days. On Fridays, they work on their scrapbooks. Each day they will be traveling they make their lunches. Then they plan the day according to bus routes and time schedules in order to make appointments or show times. At the end of each day they make notes and record their experiences.

Through interviewing key people, they have learned about city government from the mayor, about business and commerce from a bank president, and about the electronic media and entertainment field from a TV personality.

Barriers

To deal with safety concerns of both parents and staff in being on buses and out in the city, twice as many adults are assigned as required by licensing. Parents also volunteer for trips. Since the children do the planning and know that they have to be responsible, they are careful about their planning and their behavior on trips.

The children have gained self-esteem from doing their own planning and valuable independence and life skills by using the transit system.

Rewards

Children return year after year. The younger children look forward to the day they are old enough to go out on the town! The children have gained self-esteem from doing their own planning and valuable independence and life skills by using the transit system. They have been on television, in the newspaper, and have had a memorable summer.

(Adapted and reprinted by permission from BEST OF TEXAS YEARBOOK 1992© The Corporate Child Development Fund.)

(April 1993)

OLDER KIDS: BONDING OLDER KIDS TO YOUR SUMMER PROGRAM

Kids in 6th thru 9th grade are developing both interdependence and independence. It is important to win the older kids over early in your summer program if it is to be successful.

Beginning Summer Event

"Kids in 6th thru 9th grade are developing both interdependence and independence. It is important to win the older kids over early in your summer program if it is to be successful. That's why we have a special trip or event at the beginning of the summer," says Janice Baldwin, Director of the after-school program at Davidson Academy in Nashville, Tenn. And she should know. Davidson Academy is the largest school-age program under one roof in the U.S. During the school year, 430 children attend the program; most are from the 680 pre-K thru 6th grade section of the 1,230 student body pre-K thru 12th grade. In the summer 230 children attend a program that Janice starts planning almost a year ahead.

The Bonding Experience

A bonding experience can be a year long project of planning and fundraising for trips to Chicago by bus; Myrtle Beach, S.C. or St. Louis, Missouri.

But Janice points out it does not have to be an expensive or elaborate event to produce the same effects. A special camp out at a local state park or on the grounds of the school or even a Friday overnight "lock-in" provides a set of unique experiences for just that group. Experiences and stories that they can talk and laugh about that are different from what the other kids in the program have experienced.

The kids become aware that the caregivers are interested in them, not just in a paycheck (even though her staff is paid for the event). The caregivers have shown their willingness to spend extra time – it's a demonstration of commitment beyond the program.

Special Event in Early Summer Helps Bond the Other Children

Baldwin explained that they also plan a special event for everyone in the program at the beginning of summer to help show that they are significant and not just in a "day care program."

> ## Giving a new experience, especially in a setting that's new to [older kids] helps focus their energy positively.

New Experiences

Being in a setting for all day every day in the summer where the environment is the same as the after-school program, the staff is the same, and the other kids are the same means all energy for new stimulation will be focused on the one new staff person or one or two new children. Giving a new experience, especially in a setting that's new to them helps focus their energy positively.

(April 1994)

OLDER KIDS: SUMMER PROGRAMS FOR EARLY ADOLESCENTS

WHAT'S WORKING THIS SUMMER

by Rich Scofield

Recently I mentioned that there had been a higher than expected failure rate with school-age care programs for middle school children and youth and other early adolescents ages 10-15 years old. The following are two programs that have had a successful start to the summer.

A Program for 10-13 Year Olds

The Play Centers in the Baltimore, Maryland area owned and operated by Mona Criswell had successfully run their 16 school-age centers for many years. This past year they found many parents of 10-13 year olds very concerned about good, interesting summer care. So many in fact that when they had the sign up they had to split it into two programs! Each has about 60 children and youth enrolled with about 40 attending each day. (Because of family summer vacations and special family events this enrollment-attendance difference is normal in summer programs.)

Sherry Wicks is the Director of the **S.P.I.R.I.T.** program (**S**ummer **P**rograms **I**nfluencing **R**esponsibility, **I**nitiative, and **T**ogetherness). She explained that one reason the sign up was so successful was that about 75% of the kids were "alums." Play Centers was able to draw from those graduating from their other centers and those who normally might convince their parents that "this summer they were too old to go to a day care center." She estimates that about half those enrolled are kids who wouldn't have gone to Play Centers this summer.

It surprises no one in our field that S.P.I.R.I.T.'s population has an excessive number of boys, one of whom is already 6'1" tall.

What's Working So Far?

Wicks felt there were several reasons that the program is working so well besides obviously passing the first hurdle of sign-up.

- **Getting out** and about in the community at least 3 times a week.
- **Giving options** to the kids as to how the day will go and what they will do.
- **Going with the flow**.
- **Scheduling time for hanging out.**
- **Signing behavior contracts.** These are explained as being like a contract you sign when buying a car. (For young adolescents the "c" word obviously gets their attention.)
- **Gearing it to their interests.**
- **Bringing real life issues** to the program such as Drug & Alcohol counselors.
- **Electing a president of the program** who can sit in on staff meetings.

A Program for 12-15 Year Olds

The Camp on Campus Teen Camp of the Vanderbilt Child Care Center at Vanderbilt University in Nashville, TN has completed its first week of community service projects. In its first year, this community service camp is for 12-15 year olds whose parents work at Vanderbilt University (including the Hospital - a total pool of over 10,000 employees).

For several years the Child Care Center, which serves only preschoolers during the school year, has run a successful summer camp on campus for 5-12 year olds. (This year they have 80 school-agers "with tons on the waiting list.")

As many of us in this field know, desperation is the mother of invention. For Vanderbilt's Child Care Director, Jacie Dunkle, having a 12-year-old daughter who now was too old for regular school-age summer care was the impetus for starting a teen camp.

Dunkle says they started slow and small this year to ensure success and work out the problems. There are 12 youth in the program which is scheduled for four one-week sessions alternating on/off over eight weeks. Youth care is different and families can more readily accommodate the non-continuous care.

The goal of the program is to teach the youth skills for earning money, independence skills, and an introduction to volunteerism and community service.

The week just completed focused on landscaping. In the morning they learned about landscape design; how to cut grass and take care of a lawn mower; how to transplant shrubs, and set up a garden; and how to plant trees.

The service project was cutting grass, trimming lawns, and planting trees, shrubs and a garden at the homes of three senior citizens who couldn't get out to do it themselves. (They were between the ages of 85-91 years old.)

The program is supported through parent fees, University in-kind support, donated materials and special discounts such as on shrubs and plants, and support from the regular school-age summer program. Parent fees are $40 a week plus both the parent and youth have to sign up for the VU Recreation Center at $30 each for the summer. While the Rec Center plays an important role in program activities, additionally the University has lent the program a 10 bedroom student apartment as their home base. Dunkle reports they did lock all the bedrooms except the lower level to "keep an eye on things."

While initially a lot of parents signed up their teens, the kids didn't want to come. Even some of those who did come were reluctant at first - a combination of "the cool factor" and teens' general reluctance to be in new social situations. But now those same kids have signed up for the other weeks. Next year Dunkle plans to get picture posters up showing what they did this summer. She says already word of mouth has helped.

Two of the teens enrolled are from the Association for Retarded Citizens (ARC), and ARC has given the program an assistant to help with the physically challenged teens. Dunkle says having the extra adult really helps as there is only one adult available for the 12 youth in the teen camp.

The first morning everyone was trying to get past the awkwardness of the new social situation. Everybody was real shy. By noon they had all accepted each other and they were drawing straws to see who would push the kids in the wheelchairs over to the Rec Center.

Each week has a different focus with a different community service project. Each morning they pack their own lunches. Everyday after lunch they go to the VU Rec Center to play pool, racquetball, swim, etc. They have even started racquetball tournaments. Friday is a day off when they go canoeing. And they will be the leaders for a canoe trip the regular school-age camp is planning.

What are the Rules?
- Can't bring their own Walkman radios. (Radios are provided for them.)
- No hand held video games.
- Can't chew gum.
- Can't leave campus without parents' permission but can go places on campus on their own.
- **CAN** bring own books, magazines, and games. This helps add variety to their leisure hours. Also, they take good care of their own equipment!

What Makes It Successful?
- **CHOICES** - The teens have choices about recreation events, choices about their schedule and choices within the community service project.

- **CAMPUS** - Being on campus is a real plus. There is lots of outdoor shade and things to do. Also being on the University campus is "cool."
- **BEING SEPARATE** from the 5-12 year-old program camp is very important.

While having the unique recognition of being an employer-supported summer youth program, the uniqueness of the Camp on Campus for the school-age field comes from being a successful youth program born out of child care.

(July 1992)

SUMMER PROGRAMS AND YEAR-ROUND TIPS FOR WORKING WITH OLDER KIDS

by Sherry Wicks

S.P.I.R.I.T. is a Play Centers pilot program for 5th through 8th graders. Last summer was the first for the program. (See previous article) This summer we will build on the experience.

Before beginning this program, several of us sat down and tried to anticipate the challenges that would arise in caring for over 75 pre-adolescents during a ten-week period. We concluded that most pre-adolescents are at a stage of development where they will challenge anything that resembles authority.

Empowerment as a Programming Tool

We decided to hold elections at the two centers and selected a president for each. The president sat in on staff meetings and gave input regarding the success/failure of activities, trips and projects, made suggestions for future plans and was consulted on the center's budget. Apart from a few disappointed candidates, the kids generally respected and gave feedback to their president. The idea to turn the "authority" over to the kids worked for the most part. Of course, it doesn't resolve all the issues.

In the beginning of the program, we had each child sign a behavioral contract with the hope of his/her responding with compliance and respect for his/her agreement. However, one-dimensional ideas on paper don't always work out with three-dimensional pre-adolescents. As a result, we had our share of "behavior problems." Two children ran away from the center because of problems at home; one child tried to strangle another; one kid purposefully ostracized another - the list goes on. It is my contention that in order to be part of a program whose main population is 10-14 year olds, one must be ready for anything.

At this age, children are trying to establish an identity: Who am I? Where do I belong? Do people like me? In trying to discover the answers to all of these questions, the kids could be very cruel to one another.

The children judged each other on their clothes, their language, and even the way they walked. Between breaking up fights, we were drying tears. Working with this age group takes a lot of energy, creativity and perseverance.

Space to Spread Out

A concrete change that I advocated for this year is an enlarged space for the program. Although we were well within the prescribed and legal dimensions, pre-adolescents need "elbow room." I noticed last summer that, unlike preschoolers, pre-adolescents don't like others to touch them or "sit on top of" them. When one of our kids got angry or upset, it would have been ideal to have an area of the room that was quiet and allowed them to refocus. Generally, this frustrated child stayed frustrated and got in trouble.

Another challenge was the staggered entrance of the participants. Each week we had new children coming and going. Basically, the group was constantly reforming and establishing new rules and boundaries. Even though this dilemma wasn't resolvable, it helped that my staff and I were able to understand the origins of the challenges and difficulties the kids were having in constantly gaining and losing friends

What Did and Didn't Work

From the feedback I received from the kids in an end-of-summer survey, the museums/educational trips were not the greatest successes. The trips they enjoyed most were an amusement park, an adventure camp, social club, swimming, fun-in-the-sun, etc. The kids liked the trips that allowed them to express themselves physically and that allowed them to have "free-form fun." Looking back, I had the most "behavior problems" when the kids were bored or unchallenged. This year, I am not looking to exclude the "educational trips," but I am finding trips that stimulate them on both a cognitive and a physical level.

Tips for Successful Trips

I believe the kids got a lot of pleasure from the summer. Some of the most successful trips and activities were a car wash which the kids were in charge of; the trip to the amusement park (Hershey Park); the publishing of the "Dragon," the center's magazine; the election; and an Olympics. The trips and activities that were most successful had certain elements:

- The activity or trip incorporated some use of physical activity.
- The kids enjoyed the trips and activities that were new to them and that they hadn't done in school.
- It was important to the kids that they were doing something that the younger children of Play Centers couldn't do. For example, the S.P.I.R.I.T. kids decorated for the center-wide beach party and dance, ran the center-wide carnival by monitoring booths and assisting the younger kids, and were allowed to drink sodas and chew gum. This year, I hope to have a Junior Helper Day, where the S.P.I.R.I.T. kids go into other centers and become assistant counselors.

I feel the program was very successful for its first year. It provided a service to parents who might have otherwise left their older children home unattended. The kids enjoyed coming and many were reluctant to leave. We knew this because many of them lived in the neighboring areas and could walk home after 4:00 but didn't leave until 6:00 p.m. when we closed.

It takes a lot of hard work, planning, and patience to implement a program like S.P.I.R.I.T. but the rewards are endless. Regardless of the trials, tribulations and tears, S.P.I.R.I.T. Play Centers is fully committed to this program and ready to take on this summer's challengers.

(March 1993)

S.P.I.R.I.T. UPDATE

In 1993 Play Centers, Inc. completed its second summer of the **S.P.I.R.I.T.** (**S**ummer **P**rogram **I**nfluencing **R**esponsibility, **I**nitiative and **T**ogetherness) child care program for children entering fifth through eighth grades. Daily attendance ran a total of 90-100 kids at four locations. From the previous summer the program made structural changes on two levels.

Trip Fee

First, Play Centers added a trip fee of $15.00 every two weeks to the regular tuition. In general the trip fee was very well received by the members (the kids) and the parents. The parents appreciated not being asked each day for money to support various trips.

Doing their own budget

The unique aspect of this trip fee was that the members of S.P.I.R.I.T. were "in charge" of its spending. I believe the members enjoyed the opportunity to discuss financial matters. The underlying goal to be accomplished was that the members would gain some monetary skills as well as learn the value of money. By allowing the members to budget the money, it reinforced to them that the program was primarily "member-driven" [child-directed]. Many of them exceeded my expectations and were very industrious and creative in their suggestions of how to budget the money. In general the trip fee afforded the members the opportunity to go many places and gave them a chance to make some very critical and important decisions about "their" summer.

The planning process

At the beginning of the summer I outlined for the members of S.P.I.R.I.T. the general cost of some of the previous year's trips, surveyed the members as to what trips they wanted to repeat, and suggested some additional trips. The most costly of the trips was Wild World, a local amusement and water park. In order to go to Wild World, the members would have to either fund raise or limit their spending on other trips. The members decided to do both so as to allow flexibility in their spending. Like the previous summer, the members sold M&M's and held a car wash to raise extra money.

Before each trip I would tell the members of the potential cost of the trip and they would decide what extras to include. For example, the members decided how much money to spend for lunch or for the arcade and not to spend money at the Inner Harbor after visiting the National Aquarium. Approximately half-way through the summer I sat down with the presidents who had been elected earlier in the summer and presented to them the existing budget. It then became their task to review the costs before each trip with the other members. I also gave a general talk to the other members to facilitate this dialogue.

Expanding staff

The second structural change from the previous summer had been the decision to hire two directors to oversee the four locations with me "coordinating" their efforts. The program's size the previous summer had been 70 enrolled children with approximately 40-60 children on any given day at two locations. In the summer of 1993 the enrollment increased to almost 100 children with daily attendance of 90-100 members with two additional locations.

Kid survey

At the end of the summer, a survey of the members' reactions to the trips was distributed. The results supported my conclusion from the previous summer that 10-13 year olds like trips that are physically "challenging" and/or that are only available to the S.P.I.R.I.T. members (not the younger school-agers). Some of their favorites were: Cascade Lake, which has a vast swimming area, a water slide, arcades, and paddle boats; lunches at various fast food restaurants; a trip to the local mall to see a movie and shop; a trip to the local arcade; Go-Carts; and, of course, Wild World.

"Jr. Helper Day"

A special highlight from this past summer that the members said they really enjoyed was "Jr. Helper Day." During the summer Play Centers, Inc. operates approximately 11 other school-age programs (not including S.P.I.R.I.T.). The members of S.P.I.R.I.T. were offered the opportunity to go into one of the other centers that provided care for children in kindergarten through fourth grades and be "Jr. Helpers." It was explained that the Jr. Helper was responsible for creating an activity for a group of children and following-through with it in the center.

S.P.I.R.I.T. had about twenty-five "Jr. Helpers" visit different centers for approximately three hours. In that time each did his/her project and assisted the teacher. All of the members reported feeling great about their day and wishing they could have stayed longer. Some of the members expressed a new respect for the child care providers and recognized the everyday challenges that can occur.

This summer

For this coming summer the members suggested another amusement park that is two hours from the centers and an overnight trip. It will be challenging to organize and enact either of these trips. Fortunately the members of S.P.I.R.I.T. will be primarily responsible for making this happen.

In sharing with you the findings and successes of S.P.I.R.I.T.'s program, we hope you glean ideas and find encouragement in the planning of your own summer program.

(May 1994)

FIELD TRIPS: SUCCESSFUL SUMMER FIELD TRIPS

by Lauren Atwell-Douglas

So, you're faced with 10 weeks of summer, 60 children and 10-hour days—what do you do now? Before you panic, consider this: constructive field trips can enhance your summer program and provide lifelong memories for your children (after all, isn't that why we're in the business?) I emphasize constructive because anyone can plan and take a field trip. But ask yourself - will this trip benefit the children? Is it age-appropriate and are you truly prepared? If you've answered all of these questions in the affirmative, then yes, you are ready. But if there is even the slightest doubt in your mind, read on.

The smoothest running trips are those where you've adopted the Boy Scout motto, "Be Prepared."

If you're in the midst of summer camp, you've got a great resource at your disposal, namely your camp counselors. Camp counselors typically come with a predisposition to having fun, love of children and a willingness to share. As such is the case, they can be invaluable to you in helping plan and implement a field trip agenda. Set aside a portion of Counselor Orientation or staff meetings to brainstorm, plan and delegate responsibilities for a season's field trips. Giving counselors a role in planning of field trips will ensure everyone is in tune to the purpose and preparation necessary for the trip itself.

Coordinate field trips around camp themes and camper interests as this will make the experience more meaningful to the children. Counselors can prepare children for trips by relating the week's activities to a planned trip. A field trip can indeed be an enriching follow-up to any activity or theme (i.e. after studying a 4-H project on plants, take a field trip to a nature conservatory or botanical garden).

Activities during the week should be age-appropriate to increase the child's ability to relate or identify with the planned trip. Suggested activities during a week where children will visit a nature conservatory might be to have a nature walk to locate various plants, or a scavenger hunt to find as many species of leaves as possible. Enrichment studies might involve the children in keeping a pictorial journal of what they've learned about particular plants (leaf pressing will help them visualize and remember plants they've studied). Appropriate snacks during the week would be fresh vegetables and fruits (of course!). One could come up with numerous games, artwork and music related to nature. By relating field trips to camp themes, you will provide wonderful and educational memories for your campers.

Now that you've decided on which field trips you'll take and have related them to camp themes, learn as much as possible about the facility or site you've chosen to visit. By verifying admission fees, attractions related to your camp themes, group visitation policy, off-limit areas, parking and lunch accommodations, you'll save yourself countless headaches that could ruin an otherwise enjoyable experience. Calling ahead the day before your scheduled visit will also keep you abreast of changes and verify directions. Knowing these things will ultimately enable you to prepare everyone properly.

Prepare parents for field trips as far in advance as possible. Give the parents a schedule (if available) listing dates and times you'll be away from the campsite. Advise parents of departure and return times and collect permission slips (along with fees). Including a set of directions to the site of the field trip may be helpful to some parents. Encourage parents to dress their children appropriate for trips (i.e., rain gear or old clothing for hiking, etc.),. Tips on summer lunch preparation will also help parents.

To prepare your staff, give each counselor a list of children they'll be responsible for (a 1:10 ratio for school-agers is recommended). If you've been able to obtain maps of the facility, discuss meeting places, rest room locations, etc. This is also an opportune time to reiterate first aid, transportation safety rules and your camp's missing child procedures. Be prepared, and most of all, have fun!

(This article originally appeared in the June, 1991 issue of SACC Partners, published by the Southeastern Pennsylvania SACC Project. Reprinted with permission.)

(May 1996)

FIELD TRIPS: PLANNING CHECKLIST FOR FULL DAYS

by Linda G. Sisson

Programming for Full Days

When the children don't have school, you need to plan a well-paced full day of activities. Usually your group will go on a field trip on a full day. It is best to plan field trips that allow for a good deal of physical activity! The following guidelines are checklists for planning full days and field trips. The sample staff schedule shows how to use the form to show what staff should be doing at all times during a full day.

Program Coordinators' Planning Checklist for Full Days

_____ Plans formulated for "rain or shine."

_____ Reservations confirmed.

_____ Bus reserved (give bus slip and duplicate to office).

_____ Note to your supervisor with plans, times and approximate cost of admission.

_____ Letter written to parents explaining plans (have your supervisor look at the letter before you distribute it).

_____ Make the staff schedule for the day, copy, and distribute to staff.

_____ Call to reconfirm field trip reservation and plans one more time!

_____ Get plenty of rest, take your vitamins and eat a good breakfast!!!!

Timeline for Planning:

TWO WEEKS PRIOR TO THE FULL DAY: Bus reservations and field trip plans are turned into the office.

ONE WEEK PRIOR TO THE FULL DAY: Letter goes out to parents.

THE DAY BEFORE THE FULL DAY: 1) The staff schedules for the day are copied and distributed to the staff. 2) You call to reconfirm your reservation, arrival time, etc.

FIELD TRIPS:
FIELD TRIP CHECKLIST

1. Planning:

_____ Have you confirmed your reservation?

_____ Have you submitted your plans two weeks in advance to the office so they can be posted on the "master plan?"

_____ Have you arranged for payment (requested a check from the Director)?

_____ Have you informed parents (in a newsletter) of the bus times, destination, activities, and anything special the children need to bring?

_____ Have you posted a reminder a day or two ahead for parents on your bulletin board?

2. Getting Ready:

_____ Have you told the children ahead of time about the field trip? Do they know what it will involve?

_____ Have you explained to the children:

　　　1. Exactly what you expect of them on the field trip? (e.g. bus behavior, using public bathrooms, etc.)

　　　2. Whether they can keep "same seats" or not on the bus?

_____ If a child can't go on a field trip, have you made arrangements ahead of time for that child to stay with another group?

_____ Did you post a sign in your room explaining where you are and when you will be back?

_____ Have you arranged for someone to set out bags for the children's lunches if you're taking them along? And to get juice, can opener, cups, etc.?

3. Setting Off:

DO YOU HAVE...

_____ THE FIRST AID KIT WITH THE EMERGENCY CARDS

_____ THE SIGN-IN SHEET

_____ A SIGN POSTED BY YOUR ROOM

_____ WATER AND PAPER CUPS

_____ LUNCHES (IF YOU'RE GOING TO HAVE A PICNIC)

_____ JUICE (IF YOU'RE GOING TO HAVE A PICNIC)

_____ DIRECTIONS TO YOU DESTINATION

_____ YOUR GROUP CONFIRMATION

_____ PAYMENT (IF NEEDED)

AND...

_____ Did you count the children before you left, and when they got on the bus? Does the number agree with the number of children signed in for the day?

_____ Did you count the children when you got on the bus to come home?

FIELD TRIPS:
FIELD TRIP SAFETY TIPS

✪ Upon arriving at your destination, avoid herding kids in parking lots or near road by parking in the handicapped parking spaces and unloading the kids safely. Then leave a second caregiver with the kids and park the bus in a regular parking space. On leaving the area, reverse the procedure and park and load the kids from the safety of the handicapped parking spaces.

✪ Always keep the kids within your vision, be watchful for any cul-de-sac that may attract a straying child.

✪ Walk slowly on the stairs. Frequent water and bathroom stops discourage wandering.

✪ Always use partners (separating potential problems) and make the discipline or wandering problem your problem.

✪ In parks, always fish from closed bridges with lines, not poles, and using hooks with barb cut off (they'll still catch fish but catch fewer children).

✪ Keep the kids away from the banks and never near deep water.

✪ In organized playgrounds station yourself and your co-worker so all the area can be seen. Any equipment that looks too dangerous make off limits to the school-agers.

✪ Don't under or overestimate the ability of your kids; both can be dangerous.

✪ Go early in the day and preferably not on Monday or the day after a holiday as children are tired. Tired children have accidents and are not as careful as they should be, even in familiar environments.

✪ Gently drive off stray dogs, cats, squirrels, etc. Don't let kids play with unknown animals. Even if the owner of the animal is present and assures you the animal is safe, respectfully request that the kids not play with the animal.

✪ In warm weather always carry lots of water and offer it frequently.

(Adapted from Children's World Staff Newsletter)   *(March/April 1987)*

SUMMER SAFETY:
FIRST AID KITS

Two readily available first aid kits [should] be maintained by each facility, one to be taken on field trips and outings away from the site. Each kit [should] be a closed container for storing first aid supplies, accessible to child care staff members at all times but out of reach of children. First aid kits should be restocked after use, and inventory [should] be conducted at least monthly.

The first aid kit [should] contain at least the following items:

Disposable nonporous gloves

Sealed packages of alcohol wipes or antiseptic

Scissors

Tweezers

Thermometer

Bandage tape

Sterile gauze pads

Flexible roller gauze

Triangular bandages

Safety pins

Eye dressing

Pen/pencil and note pad

Syrup of ipecac

Cold pack

Current American Academy of Pediatrics or American Red Cross standard first aid text or equivalent first aid guide

Coins for use in pay phone (or access to cell phone)

Insect sting preparation

Poison control center telephone number

Water

Small plastic or metal splints

Soap

(Excerpted from Caring for Our Children, National Health and Safety Performance Standards: Guidelines for Out-of-Home Child Care Programs, *a joint collaborative project of the American Public Health Association and the American Academy of Pediatrics.)*

(May 1992)

SUMMER SAFETY:
SUNBURN, CANCER, CHILDREN:
SAC'S RESPONSIBILITY

The Problem

July and August are the two hottest months of the year north of the equator. This is a fitting time to look at ways to prevent sunburns both in staff and school-agers. Why? The evidence is mounting that sunburns during childhood and youth are related to skin cancer later in adulthood. The more skin is severely burned and the more often it is burned the greater the chance it will later become the site of skin cancer. Remember, all skin colors, from fair to dark, are susceptible to sunburn and skin cancer.

According to reports, skin cancer is the most common cancer in America, twice as common as other cancers and can be life-threatening. Two types of skin cancer, called non-melanoma, are usually not life-threatening, but tend to occur many times. The third type, melanoma, leads to death in half the cases in the U.S.

New Study

And now it has been reported that the incidence of melanoma has increased dramatically in the last 50 years, which doctors attribute in part to increased exposure to the sun. The July, 1996 issue of *Modern Medicine*, as reported by *Pediatrics for Parents*, affirms that "each time a child gets a sunburn, his chances of developing skin cancer increases."

The article cites a study of 1,825 children cared for in 16 different Chicago-area child care centers, which found that 60% of the children were never properly protected against sunburn, in spite of the fact that the children were most often sent outside during the sunniest times of the day. Only 25% of the children occasionally had sunscreen applied on their skin before going outside.

Most teachers stated that they didn't apply the sunscreen because it was too much trouble. However, interestingly, some child care administrators stated a fear of litigation for their reason not to apply sunscreen. The report states that these administrators "consider suncreen a 'medication,' and no medication can be 'given' to a child without parental authorization."

SAC staff have a responsibility to minimize children's exposure to sunburn and fast tanning (a tan is the skin's response to injury). Rather than worry about litigation related to applying a medication, it seems more likely that a program that lets children "fry" in the sun without consideration of protection would be negligent and open to being sued. Certainly, staff feeling it is "too much trouble" is not a reason to leave children unprotected.

SAC programs and staff need to have policies and procedures that protect children from both sunburn and heat stroke. These should be just as much a responsibility in SAC as any other health and safety issue. See the following article on "Sun Tips" for ideas for your policies and procedures.

(June 1997)

SUMMER SAFETY: SUN TIPS

How do other programs handle the issue of sun protection and what are some of the tips and strategies you should consider for your policies and procedures?

School-Age NOTES phoned around to find out what other programs do about this. One large multi-site program in Florida does not have an explicit policy about sunscreen. But the director reminded us that in the summer in Florida most people stay in the air-conditioned buildings and only venture outside before 10 a.m. and after 4 p.m. Parents and kids are fairly "sun savvy" and do things like wear t-shirts when swimming.

A multi-site program in Minnesota has guidelines for parents to provide sunscreens and for staff to be diligent about kids covering up and to monitor how much sun and heat they are exposed to. Some of the things they do are:

- ❏ Have kids keep their sunscreen in their cubbies.
- ❏ Have on hand a "kids brand" sun block, safe enough even for infants, for those kids without sunscreen.
- ❏ Create a routine putting on their sunscreen (and hats and sunglasses) each time before going outside.
- ❏ Check and help the kids who may have problems getting covered.
- ❏ Limit to about one hour the time kids are continuously exposed.
- ❏ Don't let kids run around with their shirts off.

If outside the whole day (on field trip or special events day), they:

❏ Have kids drink plenty of water.
❏ Bring own water, don't rely on having water available at the destination site.
❏ Make kids take breaks in the shade and time to cool down.

General Tips

Here are more sun-safety tips that your program can use:

❏ **Alert** parents and staff to the dangers of sun exposure and your program's concern. Ask parents for their help in protecting their children.

❏ **Inform** staff, parents, and children of your efforts to help prevent over-exposure to the sun.

❏ **Remember** ultraviolet rays from sunlight, which cause cancer, can reach the skin on cloudy days and even underwater.

❏ **Minimize the time** children are on the playground between 10 a.m. and 2 p.m. which is the most intense period of ultraviolet rays.

❏ **Encourage children** to wear hats and sunscreens or sunblock lotions when on the playground or on field trips, particularly when around pools or beaches.

❏ **Help parents** raise this issue with school systems regarding lunch recess outside and outdoor field trips and picnics. This is particularly important in the summer for year-round systems or for schools in tropical climates.

❏ **Have staff model** good sun protection techniques.

(June 1997)

SUMMER SAFETY:
SUMMER SUN ALERT

It's that time of year when staff at all day summer programs have to be aware of the need to protect school-agers skin from too much sun. The American Cancer Society has stated that even one severe sunburn can double children's chances of getting skin cancer at some point in their lives, even if it's 40 or 50 years later. And cases of skin cancer are increasing by 12% per year.

Some of the issues for programs in knowing when and how to apply sunscreen to their charges include:

● getting 30-50 children adequately covered before letting them go outside
● potential skin allergies to some sunscreens
● reapplication after excessive sweating or after being in the pool
● individual state regulations concerning sunscreen application

For example, the Colorado Day Care Rules & Regulations #62D concerning sun protection state that:

1. The center must obtain the parent or guardian's written authorization and instructions for applying sunscreen to their children's exposed skin prior to outside play. A doctor's permission is not needed to use sunscreen at the center.

2. When supplied for an individual child, the sunscreen must be labeled with the child's first and last name.

3. If sunscreen is provided by the center, parents must be notified in advance, in writing, of the type of sunscreen the center will use.

4. Children over 4 years of age may apply sunscreen to themselves under the direct supervision of a staff member.

Also in Colorado, child care centers assume liability for a child's severe sunburn and it may be considered neglect by Child Protection Services.

Programs should determine whether there are regulations in their state concerning applying sunscreen to children in child care programs, as well as be aware of general principles concerning the application of sunscreen:

✔ The skin must be completely dry and cool in order for the sunscreen to adhere. Children just coming out of the pool or who are sweaty will still be in danger of sunburn if sunscreen is applied when the skin is not dry or cool to the touch.

✔ The initial application of sunscreen is most important. Apply sunscreen thoroughly on cool, dry skin and all areas that will be exposed to the sun.

✔ Take your time and be sure the first application is complete. Also be sure that you can feel a layer of sunscreen between your hands and the skin where sunscreen is being applied.

✔ Apply sunscreen at least 10-30 minutes before sun exposure.

✔ Reapply sunscreen after swimming, toweling off, or heavy sweating. Waterproof sunscreens means only that the sunscreen stays on your skin for 80 minutes while immersed in water.

✔ Children with very fair, sensitive skin must wear sunscreen and should also wear long sleeve shirts and wide brim hats if exposure to the sun will be prolonged. It's actually a good idea for all children and staff to wear hats for extended periods outdoors.

✔ Avoid going on outdoor field trips, going swimming or having outside play in sunny areas from 10 a.m. - 2 p.m.

(June 1999)

GUIDANCE:
GROUP MANAGEMENT IDEAS

The following are some basic group management tips:

- ✔ Develop a well-rounded, interesting program - plan, plan, plan!
- ✔ Keep rules to a minimum, but consistently enforce them.
- ✔ Allow children to participate in the decision-making process of both rules and consequences of infractions.
- ✔ Plan the environment to avoid congestion and allow for smooth transitions.
- ✔ Use routines to help children with transitions but remember the importance of being flexible.
- ✔ State expectations positively - "We will walk in the halls," rather than the negative "No running in the halls."
- ✔ Be sure rules and routines are understood by all.
- ✔ Be fair and reasonable in your expectations.
- ✔ Listen seriously to and give feedback on children's ideas, questions, and concerns.
- ✔ Stress the positive in each situation. Rather than "Julio, you forgot the cups!" try, "Thank you Julio, for bringing the plates, forks and napkins. We also need some cups; would you get them, please?"
- ✔ Build self-confidence and self-esteem rather than using destructive sarcasm, belittling, or other verbal abuse.
- ✔ Help provide children with the security of structure and boundaries by setting clear limits, firmly defined and enforced but flexible enough to meet individual needs.

GUIDANCE: TIME FOR "TIME-OUT" TO RETIRE

LET BALANCE CENTER TAKE ITS PLACE

by Sue Lawyer-Tarr

If time-out could talk, he'd say: "I've been misused and abused and accumulated too much emotional baggage through the years. I need to be replaced!" Let's enter the 21st Century with "Balance Centers." A Balance Center is a quiet space away from the maddening crowd and heat of action, where tired, angry, sad or aggressive children may go to regroup, recoup, recenter, and regain their balance. Entry into the Balance Center requires three deep long exaggerated breaths that immediately help a child center and re-focus. This helps a child let go of what he's been resisting feeling so he can be "present" and attend to solutions. Once inside a child will find soft pillows or bean bag chairs and a box full of items to help him regain his composure.

> **A Balance Center is a quiet space away from the maddening crowd and heat of action, where tired, angry, sad or aggressive children may go to regroup, recoup, recenter, and regain their balance.**

Most important when a child first enters the Balance Center, kind, quiet words are spoken by a staff person about what might be of help to the child in regaining his balance. "Johnny, when I'm angry or upset, it helps me to draw what I'm feeling or just make funny faces into my mirror for a few minutes. I know if I do anything when I'm that angry, I'll only make a bigger problem. This box is full of tools that can be of help to you. Why don't you take a look inside and see what you think would help you right now."

Your center can create a "Balance Box" out of an empty copy paper box. Children like to collage the box with words like kindness, compassion, and joy and find or draw pictures that demonstrate these words. What will children find in the box?

1. A clipboard with paper, pencils, crayons; several small journals made from recycled paper.
2. A small heavy plastic glove filled with fine sand to feel and squeeze.
3. A Koosh ball, a stress squeeze ball, a few Toobers and Zots, and a Slinky.
4. A quarter size ball of beeswax to warm in the hand to shape and reshape.
5. An unbreakable mirror for making faces and looking deep inside themselves.
6. A small cassette headset with cassettes of ocean, wind, or forest sounds, or Indian flutes.
7. Several short, easy-to-read books about handling our ups and downs and disagreements.
8. A laminated picture of 30 faces expressing all sorts of feelings, with a word expressing the emotion to help a child identify his or her own feelings. What a child can't speak she acts out.
9. Several different types of conflict resolution Q & A forms for a child to choose from.
10. A cassette recorder and blank tape for children to use while discussing solutions to conflicts with one another. The focus is on "feeling" talk to develop empathy and solutions to problems. Staff encourage children to make eye contact with one another and discuss "what will work," and "help instead of hurt."
11. A kaleidoscope to look through. Concentric patterns help balance the brain's right and left hemispheres. Also, mandala ink drawings, concentric patterns for children, are very centering and calming.
12. Stories and poems about how others resolve conflicts and face difficult emotions.
13. *The Warm Fuzzy Tale*, by Claude Steiner (based on Transactional Analysis). Children love this book and relate well to its principles of warm fuzzies and cold pricklies. (Create your own warm fuzzies out of velvety pompom balls; sweet gum tree balls make great cold pricklies.)
14. A laminated 5x7 card that says, "Pray for God's Help and Guidance."

If a child is not willing to participate in the Balance Center to help himself/herself self-correct when his/her actions are dangerous or very disruptive, a meeting with the child and his/her parents needs to be held. Remember that democracy is not anarchy, and freedom is not license. When a child is being a tyrant, (playing I win, you lose), an adult speaking with authority and setting boundaries, limits and consequences is very clearly called for. Staff who are permissive, ignore inappropriate behavior and avoid conflict, are, by default, teaching children to dominate, manipulate and control instead of looking for win/win solutions. At the beginning of the family conference, ask Johnny to explain why this meeting has been called. This provides valuable information for staff as to how the child views the problem and insight into how Johnny interacts with his parents and his family with him. After the child has completed describing the problem you are trying to solve, staff can then fill in any important facts that may have been omitted. Parents are then asked to support their child in making any necessary corrections. The actions the child needs to take need to be spoken very clearly by staff. Again, our focus is always on solutions and win/win outcomes. Staff ask Johnny what inappropriate actions he will commit to change, and what support he may need from us to do this. We ask Johnny to state in his own words, the actions he thinks will solve this problem. If a child's aggressive or tyrannical behavior continues, staff will need to look at whether the other children's safety and well-being is being compromised by allowing this child to continue in the program. Referring parents to a guidance counselor for help may be the next step to take. These actions are usually all that is required to help a child self-correct without being dismissed from the program.

What we now can say is, "Good-bye 'time-out!' Although you may have started out with good intentions, you have become quite a dictator." Balance Centers are an effective way of empowering children in a democracy.

Sue Lawyer-Tarr is a national school-age consultant and workshop leader and author. She opened her after-school program "The Clubhouse After School Caring and Sharing" in 1977 and has received local and national recognition for the program's excellence. She has authored two books, How to Work with School-Age Children and Love Them *and* School-Age Child Care Professional Training: A Workbook for Teaching Staff.

(April 1999)

GUIDANCE:
SUFFERING SIBLINGS

by Tracy Besley

George, Akosua, & Jonathan:
George, 10, and Akosua, 9, follow Jonathan, 5, everywhere and run interference for him with other children. They make sure he gets the toys he wants and that no one takes them away from him. They have instructions from their mom to hit anyone who hurts Jon.

Rusty, Ronnie, & Ruth:
Now eight-years-old, Rusty, Ronnie, and Ruth, triplets, argue and bicker almost constantly. They bring lunch in one big container and fight over having to share.

During the summer many programs have more sibling pairs and trios. School-agers, whose parents may have felt okay to leave them at home alone after school, are now needing all-day supervision. Increasingly, parents are looking for summer supervision for children as old as ninth grade. Siblings in the same program add a challenge, especially if one or more of the siblings is a teen.

How to surmount the summer-sibling scene and still have sanity when school starts? One of the things that has helped me is a book called *Siblings Without Rivalry*, by Adele Faber and Elaine Mazlish.

"The first step toward coping with siblings [is] giving up the expectation that [they] are going to behave reasonably toward one another simply because they are related."

My first experience with siblings was with my own brother and sisters. I came to believe that I did not have much in common with them except having the same parents. I decided that given a choice, I probably would not choose my siblings as my friends. Faber and Mazlish write:

"Instead of worrying about siblings becoming friends, [we] began to think about how to equip them with the attitudes and skills they'd need for all their caring relationships. There was so much for them to know. [We] didn't want them hung up all their lives on who was right and who was wrong. [We] wanted them to be able to move past that kind of thinking and learn how to really listen to each other, how to respect the differences between them, how to find ways to resolve differences. Even if their personalities were such that they never could be friends, at least they would have the power to make a friend or be a friend."

So the first step toward coping with siblings, for me, was giving up the expectation that siblings are going to behave reasonably toward one another simply because they are related. When I let go of this expectation, I was able to allow their negative feelings toward each other. Before, I would deny their feelings with comments like "But she's your sister!" or "How could you? He's your brother!"

Faber and Mazlish point out a puzzling paradox:

"Insisting upon good feelings between siblings led to bad feelings. *Allowing* (emphasis added) bad feelings led to good feelings."

I learned the hard way, as the authors point out, the importance of treating each child as a unique individual and avoiding comparisons. Whether favorable or unfavorable, comparisons cause unhappiness. Instead of: "Why can't you hang up your clothes like your brother?" try describing what you see, "I see your jacket on the floor." Or, describe what you feel, "That bothers me." Or describe what needs to be done, "The jacket belongs in the closet." Instead of: "You're much neater than your brother," speak only about the behavior that pleases you. Describe what you see, "I see you hung up your jacket." Or, describe what you feel, "I appreciate that. I like seeing our hallway looking neat."

The key though, is to remember that each sibling is special and unique and to treat them that way.

(May 1988)

GUIDANCE:
GOOD TERMINATION POLICIES

A Plus for Kids, Programs, and Families
by Dale Fink

Any termination policy answers two questions: (1) What are the behaviors that could lead to termination? (2) When someone engages in these behaviors, what procedures will be followed?

In answering the first question, we set boundaries that are helpful in promoting good discipline. Families benefit from understanding the behaviors that can jeopardize their children's participation. Children with attention and behavioral problems benefit from the clearest possible demarcation of limits.

In answering the second question, we create mechanisms to ensure that everyone is treated fairly and that other solutions are fully explored prior to terminating a child's participation. This article explores three principles that might be followed in designing a termination policy.

> ## We terminate due to the behaviors, not because "we are unable to meet the needs of the child."

First Principle: Observable Behaviors are the Yardstick

Termination must be based on specific observable behaviors. We may believe that unacceptable behaviors are a result of unmet needs, but we terminate due to the behaviors, not because "we are unable to meet the needs of the child."

In our printed policies we should identify the kinds of behaviors that can lead to termination. These might include unprovoked physical violence, persistent bullying, verbal harassment of peers or staff, and unauthorized departure from the grounds of the program. When problems arise with a particular child, we should spell out on paper the specific behaviors that are problematic so there is no danger of the child or family misinterpreting our expectations. For instance, "Jess will not place his hands on another child's neck or face unless they have asked him to do so." I would caution against using such phrases as "Jess will act in a cooperative manner," or "Jess will be respectful of staff." "Cooperative" and "respectful" are states of mind, not observable behaviors, and are open to differences in interpretation.

Second Principle: The Behavior (Not the Child or Parent) is Our Antagonist

We have only one antagonist in this conflict: the unacceptable behaviors. To figure out why the child is engaging in these behaviors and to bring an end to them is a joint enterprise requiring the creative thinking of the child, the parents, and ourselves. It is not a confrontation between ourselves and the child or between ourselves and the family. We will succeed together with the family and assure the child's continued participation, or fail together – and terminate.

How do we implement this principle? We not only keep parents informed of a child's problematic behaviors but also convey our expectations about their role. What do we want from parents? First, their insights into what may be at the root of the behaviors. Second, their ideas or strategies to help us. (If the child has special needs, this would include help in communicating with specialists or in accessing resources.) Third, a commitment to sit down periodically and brainstorm together.

Without our guidance, many parents will take feedback about a child's behavior to mean they are expected to "fix" the problem – often by punishing the child. They are usually relieved to find out that we are not blaming them for the problems and not holding them solely responsible for the solution.

As much as possible, the process we go through with the parents should also be open to the child. On days you are meeting with her parent(s), sit down informally with Daphne. "Do you understand why I've asked your dad to come and talk with me?" "Do you know which behaviors of yours we are concerned about?" "Do you have any suggestions for how we can help you to change your behavior?" "Would you like to come to our meeting and talk about it?" Invite her to be present for a portion of the parent-teacher meeting. Explain this part of your policy to the parent in advance, and make sure the parent gets a chance to say everything he wanted to say outside the child's earshot before you invite Daphne into the meeting.

Third Principle: Programming Before Dismissal

What are the outcomes of the brainstorming among staff and with parents? If you simply spell out a series of increasingly harsh disciplinary sanctions, culminating in termination, then you have forgotten your aspirations to high quality. Your termination policy should commit you to trying out programming changes that will better engage the interests and abilities of the child, and to help her make friends. The *NSACA Standards for Quality School-Age Care* (1998) call on us to "help children find ways to pursue their own interests," "encourage children to take leadership roles," and "give children many chances to choose what they will do, how they will do it, and with whom." Whenever a child is not meeting our behavioral expectations, we should ask whether we have done all we can to shape the program in ways that engage this particular child's attentions and energy – before we go farther along the pathway of punishment.

In the case of a child with a disability, such program alterations are a legal obligation. We are required under the Americans with Disabilities Act (ADA) to make "reasonable modifications" to meet the needs of any child with disabilities (including ADD or ADHD). If we receive federal funds (e.g., federal nutrition program), we are also subject to Section 504, with a similar requirement for program accessibility. These concepts do not refer only to the removal of architectural barriers but to modifying activity choices, room arrangement, social groupings, or daily schedules — in short, any elements of our program that might detract from a child's ability to participate successfully. We must document all the program modifications we tried prior to terminating the enrollment of a child with a disability.

While even contemplating the need for termination policies can be difficult for many program directors, they are important. When handled carefully, these policies can help children, families, and programs avoid being buried by behavior problems.

(Dale Fink is a free-lance writer and consultant who has been a featured speaker at school-age conferences from New England to New South Wales (Australia). His book Discipline in School-Age Care: Control the Climate, Not the Children *is available from School-Age NOTES. Contact him at P.O. Box 363, Williamstown MA 01267, fax or phone at 413-458-5334 or email at finkdale@sover.net.)*

(April 2000)

ACTIVITIES:
GARDENING: NOW AND DURING SUMMER

Here are some ideas related to helping children learn more about land, about soil, water, sun, bugs, flowers, vegetables and other green stuff. All of these ideas can be done independent of each other or in preparation for a summer garden.

✿ Have the children order seed catalogs from several companies (Burpee and Park Seed are two popular companies.) The kids can look through the catalogs, choosing what flowers and vegetables they'd like to grow. Help the children find out what grows best in your area.

✿ Visit a full-line plant and garden nursery or feed store. Find out about tools, soil additives, seeds/plants, and fertilizers.

✿ Arrange a visit to your local Agricultural Center. Bring a sample of soil to be tested. What nutrients are missing? How do you replace those missing nutrients? You may want a representative to visit your site to discuss the best spot for your garden.

✿ Start seedlings indoors.

✿ Sprout a plant.

✿ Plan a garden on paper. Teach the kids to draw it to scale on graph paper.

No suitable spot? Not enough land? No summer program? Alternatives to providing gardening experiences when limitations exist are:

✿ Grow plants indoors in big tubs.

✿ Cooperate with another agency (community center, church, senior citizen center, or even a private home) or with another person (volunteer, board member, parent) to work on a garden together. Be honest with what you can contribute and what you cannot. Decide who will do what and how. Decide how you will share the garden bounty.

✿ Grow seedlings at the program for children to plant at home. Be sure to find out, put in writing and send home instructions on how to plant and care for seedlings.

✿ Plant fruits, vegetables, flowers that will bloom and mature before summer begins. You can speed this process by using a miniature greenhouse indoors.

(March/April 1985)

ACTIVITIES:
SUMMER OVERNIGHT CAMPING

by Vivan Mannis

Many national parks and recreation areas have free programs that invite community groups to use park facilities. Our experience with the Gateway National Recreation areas located on the border of a densely populated urban area provided a "get away" for children and leaders, and exposure to outdoor living experiences which were rewarding to all.

During the past two summers more than thirty 8- to 10-year-old children and four staff members from the "Juniors" School-Age Program at the Hi Hello Child Day Care Center in Freeport, New York, spent two fun-filled, exciting days and one night experiencing living at the Gateway National Recreation Area in Brooklyn. They learned the art of tent pitching, detritus preservation, seining (two people fishing with one net) and organic gardening.

Planning for the "overnight" began in the early spring. Three leaders spent a training weekend at the park. They learned about the program for children, what [our school-age program] would need to provide, how meals and routines would be handled. All the time and effort really paid off. The children had a wonderful time and learned a great deal, too!

Some of the children's own comments:

"I learned how to tell poison ivy by the leaves. The poison ivy has three leaves and is shiny."

"In the morning we went to the garden, we picked vegetables and ate them, then we had lunch."

"I learned how to cut the weeds in the garden. We also went fishing in Jamaica Bay. We caught whiting, jellyfish and mud snails."

"I liked wearing the waders and using the seining net. I learned how to put up a tent and how to cook outdoors. We had a great time!"

"In case you are wondering about what the food chain is, I will tell you: It is started by the sun (we all know there would not be life without the sun). It produces food for animals which are killed by people and become food for people."

"We had to sleep in pup tents, they are very small. At night most of the kids ran out of the tents. We moved one of the tents. At night when we got caught in the rain it wasn't that bad. We went inside in the main building where we played with the earthball."

An unexpected bonus — leaders and children can't wait until NEXT summer to go camping — a new Hi Hello tradition!

There are campgrounds managed by scout groups and other outdoor organizations which are available at little or no cost for overnight trips all year. Get in touch with the outdoor groups in your area!

(March/April 1984)

ACTIVITIES:
CAN YOU CARRY IT?

Every summer, a brave child care worker decides to take the school-agers on an overnight camping trip. And every summer at least one (if not more) school-ager packs every possession she owns for the trip. The scene goes like this:

Child care worker to school-agers: "Pack only enough for one night, and only what you can carry. We'll be hiking half a mile from where we park the van and it's all uphill!"

On the day of the overnight, Jasmine, age 10, arrives with two suitcases, one duffel bag, one backpack, and two paper bags. "Jasmine," cautions the still brave but now amazed child care worker, "Remember you have to carry all that half a mile uphill. Everyone has to carry their own stuff. You'd better leave some of that here." At that Jasmine wails, "I can't. I need everything." Brave, amazed but naively sweet child care worker says, "Okay, Jasmine, but remember you have to carry it all yourself."

As you can guess by now, Jasmine can be seen struggling with her possessions, wailing for someone to help her, refusing to take one more step, crying to go home, and creating misery for herself and others.

Is there any way around this ever-recurring problem scene? YES!

Act It Out

School-agers learn best by doing. Therefore a mock trip to the campsite can help school-agers to know how much they can carry or how much is too much.

How to Do A Mock Trip

1. Collect several pillows, sleeping bags, old suitcases (filled with books to equal weight of camp gear), "mess" kit, and stuffed dufflebags and back packs.
2. Give each child the opportunity to carry a pillow, sleeping bag, suitcase and "mess" kit around the room several times (equal to approximately the distance from the van to the campsite.)
3. Talk it out after the mock trips. Did you get tired? Was it heavy? If not, try carrying two suitcases! Did you wish someone could help carry your things? How much can you carry by yourself?

School-agers may now be prepared to make a list of things they will need. This list can be carried home to help in packing and brought to camp for checking off belongings when going home. The list helps limit but also serves as a reminder for essential items. (If you feel it helpful, another list can be made of the things to be left at home. Example: teddy bears, radios, gum…)

This mock trip idea can be used in other situations where school-agers need the actual doing of the experience to understand what will and won't work. As people move into adolescence and adulthood, they often can do "mock" trips in their heads to figure out what works, but school-agers need the concreteness — the actual doing — to understand.

Try "mock" experiences for expected behavior on field trips to museums or theaters, or for preparation for emergencies such as fires.

(May/June 1985)

ACTIVITIES:
KIDS AND MONEY

The long days of summer are often viewed with dread by caregivers. How can I plan for something all day, every day? While the very young school-agers are content with their repetitive play and the middle school-agers are relatively involved with secret groups and budding peer social systems, the older school-agers' complaint is boredom.

Developmentally the pre-adolescent (starting around 10-years-old or 5th grade) becomes very interested in money. While to parents it seems as though they are only interested in spending it, they are very interested in how to get it.

Summer provides an excellent time to introduce the idea of creating money-making projects. During the school year, one is always aware of the short amount of time each afternoon to work on long range projects. Summer provides an opportunity for a designated block of time, 10 to 12 weeks, during which the children have ample time during the days to plan and implement their ideas.

Money and earning money will attract all ages of children in your school-age program. However, it is the older children who have the cognitive and academic ability to persevere with such projects. They can retain long term goals (working hard now to make more later, or saving up now to buy something later). The value of money and its purchasing power is well set. (While the 5-year-old will choose 15 pennies over 2 dimes because it "looks" like more, the older school-ager will feel insulted if asked to make that choice.) The older children have the math skills (or will soon want to) to divide net profits after adding up gross profits and subtracting expenses.

Developmentally, the older child has a desire to earn money. The 10-12-year-old has started to progress past the 8-9-year-old who is content with doing adult-type tasks just for the sake of "real tools, real work." This older child now is beginning to connect the reasons for doing things with a sense for the future. (We clean the kitchen to keep the bugs out and to prevent sickness. My parent has to work to earn money to feed and clothe us.)

Not only are the children developmentally ready to learn about money in a real way, but the nation seems ready to teach children this. A big push toward economics in the upper grades and junior highs is emerging. Grants are being given to colleges to develop plans to teach children economics — *children in the world of work.* That phrase may strike a chord of vague ill ease because of the images of children in "sweat shops" which brought about child labor laws in this country. While in many countries children are still forced to work (and it still needs to be guarded against in this country) letting them plan their own money-making projects is a way of meeting their developmental needs. It also follows the tradition of the lemonade stand and newspaper route.

Ideas

Motivation - while there's plenty of it at the outset when it comes to making money, it must be clear from the beginning the **goal** for the project – that is — who gets the profits, why are you raising money? It may be for something big— a camping trip, an expensive day trip (these can be planned as end of the summer events) — or for something smaller — a trip to the movies, a new kickball, a surprise gift for the director of the center/minister of the church/principal of the school.

Some programs choose to let the children split the profits among themselves just as if they were at home with their lemonade stand.

Remember to include the younger children in the process. Think of what they can do within their age range to help. The 5 and 6-year-olds can help with the art work for posters. The 7-year-olds can be the "gofors" running messages and getting needed items. The 8 and 9-year-olds can help with the list-making and record-keeping while the older children are "in charge" of the money as well as directing the project.

While the emphasis has been on the older children and their ability and desire to make money, those programs with primarily younger grade children can also conduct money-making projects. However, it should be remembered that the younger the children, the more adult help in planning and implementation will be needed.

Project ideas can include car washes, bake sales, pancake breakfasts, plays, magic and puppet shows, collecting newspapers and aluminum cans, helping local business people (sweeping sidewalks in the morning, etc.)

Family day homes can look around their neighborhood for people who may want help with mowing lawns, carrying groceries or cleaning out storage areas.

(May/June 1981)

ACTIVITIES: NEWSLETTERS

Fun, Learning, & Parent Communication

A weekly or bi-weekly newsletter during the summer, prepared by the children can be an exciting activity and learning experience. It also can serve to communicate to parents both important dates and give them a sense of what their children are doing this summer (or during the school year).

How to Do It

✍ Older children can be reporters and scribes. (Handprinted newsletters with lots of the children's names and drawings are more likely to be read by parents than typed ones.)

✍ Younger children can contribute drawings and be interviewed.

✍ Adults should help with ideas on general layout to keep it simple and attractive. (Use lines to separate sections. Leave white space on edges and between sections.)

✍ Ideas include interviews, jokes, parent surveys (Questions for parents such as "What did you like to do most when you were in elementary school?" "What did you do for fun?", etc.). Also encourage parent participation through ideas such as a Parent Corner — solicit summer recipes, ideas for vacations on a shoestring budget, etc. This section can be typed in.

✍ Don't worry about errors, misspellings, lopsided drawings, and fingerprints. It is that kind of "cuteness" that makes parents and others read it. Of course, your school-age editors might demand perfection.

✍ Printing it: — 1 or 2 sheets both sides printed will do (legal size paper helps because the drawings and printing take up space).

— Copy machines are in many agencies - see if you can use it if you provide the paper. Some areas have very low cost quick copy shops. Also see if businesses want to donate copying as a contribution.

— Vary color of paper if possible.

✍ Take advantage of children's interest in money-making projects by having them sell the newsletter (which can help defray costs.)

✍ Related ideas — trips to printing companies and local newspapers

Ideas contributed by "The City Road Kids" newsletter, Madison, TN

(May/June 1982)

ACTIVITIES:
HOW TO ORGANIZE CLUBS, EVEN WITHOUT EXTRA SPACE OR STAFF

by Tracey Ballas and Flo Reinmuth

"Clubs for older kids sounds like a terrific idea." says Barb, a school-age child care worker, "But every time we try to organize a club the kids lose interest, start to fight or leave someone out and then we have hurt feelings. Besides that, we just don't have the space and even if we did, we would not have enough staff to supervise the group."

How do we go about accomplishing this task of organizing a club that does not end up causing us more problems? How do we provide the necessary staff and space to accommodate these kids?

The first step is to determine the space and staffing for the club. Several options exist that can work best for your program.

In a facility that is exclusively for child care, designating a separate room for the older children and assigning staff to the group is more easily accomplished. However, in a shared small space situation, try these alternatives:

✪ Partition off a part of the room for the use of the club. This can be done by using something as simple as a coat rack and hang a shower curtain on it so the older children can have privacy.

If you are housed in a cafeteria, use the tables as dividers. This area can be set up and taken down each day. Within these spaces, keep supplies that are just for the older school-agers such as: radio/tape player; pre-teen magazines; Legos; bean bags.

✪ Designate 2 or 3 days a week to be "club day." Assign one staff member to supervise and set up the club in another room. This situation suits a program that has limited space and staff, enabling the program to provide a club on a part-time basis.

✪ Institute a program such as Big Brother/Big Sister or Kings/Queens. Although there is no designated space, they are entitled to special privileges and activities. For example, club kids don't have to attend the general meeting that is held at the beginning of the program. Or, if they do attend, they may sit on the table instead of the floor.

✪ Develop fun sheets and challenges in magic tricks just for them. Enhance the BB/BS aspect by designing activities that must be done with a younger school-ager. Completion of these special activities warrants a token. At the end of one month, they can trade their tokens in for either an extra privilege or prize.

The next step is to convene a meeting of the interested older school-agers:

Emphasize the responsibilities of being a member of this club. Begin by stating the guidelines of the club and the need for ownership by the members. The guidelines can be presented in a packet form*, however, these are only guidelines and the students must have input or the club will not survive.

Allow club members to:

— Choose a name for the club

— Elect representatives who will be responsible for organizing events and activities that the members choose to do

— Create their own rules, as well as follow non-negotiable program rules.

Work through the organization process slowly with the older kids. Keep meetings brief (15 to 20 minutes). Once members feel ownership of their club, staff will say, "Yes, clubs are terrific for the older kids!"

* Packets for older kids' clubs can include: 1. Guidelines; 2. Club information sheet; 3. Rules, with space left to fill in their own created rules; 4. Club agreement or contract signed by parent and child; 5. Club "rep" form; 6. Club evaluation form; and 7. Club description and information form (for the program's and club's newsletter).

(November/December 1989)

Page 100 offers a sample "Club Information Sheet" originally developed by Edina (Minn.) Kids Club staff and slightly adapted for School-Age NOTES.

WELCOME TO THE CLUB

Welcome

It's great to have you as a member of our club. Being in the 3rd, 4th, and 5th grade entitles you to be a club member — a special group of kids with privileges and opportunities not available to the younger children. This paper will help you find out more about what it takes to be a member in the club.

What We're Here For/What You're Here For

The club is here to provide a place where you, an older kid, can feel at home — a place to relax, make friends, and enjoy doing those things you like to while developing confidence, independence and respect for yourself and others.

Freedom and Supervision

Being a club member means you will be able to make a lot of choices about how you spend your time at the school-age program. We will provide as many opportunities as possible. Because you are older now, we feel you do not need direct adult supervision at all times. We and your parents are going to be trusting you a lot to act properly and respectfully both when leaders are present and when they are not.

The most important thing we do ask of you is that you always let us know where you will be at all times. You do this verbally and through the check-out system. That is, when you go to another area either with an adult or with just a few other kids, you must place a card in your mail pouch indicating where you are going to be. On return to the club area, remove the card.

Communication

Read the bulletin boards each day for updates on activities and special events. A lot of information on what's happening at the club will be in the club newsletters sent to your family. You are responsible for reading notices.

Input

The club staff depends on you to help plan special events, programs and activities for your group. Your initiative, ideas, and suggestions are welcome!! Your creativity and energy will help make a GREAT club every day.

(November/December 1989)

ACTIVITIES:
SUMMER READING

USA Today reports that kids who do not read during the summer "drop back at least six months," quoting Bernice Cullinan, author of *Read to Me: Raising Kids Who Love to Read*. No research is cited but the article also quoted Elizabeth Segal, author of *For Reading Out Loud!*, that kids who read as little as 15 minutes a day can advance their reading level by up to 5 months. Their advice is to make reading materials available everywhere, and possibly read a first chapter aloud to whet an interest.

Recreational reading need not be at the highest reading level the child has achieved in order to be of value. Besides good books on the shelf and opportunities to read them, try some of these:

❂ Read aloud a chapter a day. When you stop for the day, ask, "What do you think will happen next?" and "We'll find out tomorrow." Or whet interest in a book by reading just one chapter and then putting the book back on the free reading shelf.

❂ Make a book into a drama. Read for clues to describe each character. Decide which scenes to include and read for descriptions of costumes and settings. Make a list of hand props you will need. Write a script based on dialogue in the book. Break up these assignments so each committee is reading for something different.

❂ Share a book with outstanding illustrations. Then read a book with no illustrations or with only a few. Decide which scenes in the book you would like to illustrate. Read for descriptions of characters and settings. Make your illustrations as true to the text as you can, but allow for imagination.

❂ Make a poster of a book you have read that would make someone else want to read it.

❂ Have a storybook day and dress up as a character from a book you have read this summer.

❂ Try out dialects. Read aloud a story in which at least one character (if not the storyteller) speaks in a dialect. Let everyone try out the dialect. What does the dialect tell you about the character? Decide whether the dialect adds to the character and to the story and makes it more like drama or just makes it hard to read. Be sensitive to people's feelings about their dialects and help children avoid using dialects to make fun of people.

(June 1993)

ACTIVITIES:
STORYTELLING:
ANYONE CAN DO IT!

by Gay Ducey

Okay. The field trip is over. The bus is late. Some of the kids are sunburned, and the rest are mad. What do you do? You pull out the most effective and portable of all educational experiences: you tell a story. You are amazed to find that it quiets even the most obstreperous child. Well, you may be surprised, but I am not. I am a professional storyteller, and I see its magic everyday.

Storytelling is the entertainment that teaches, and the school-age program is a natural setting for it. When you put down the book, and simply tell the story, you are giving kids more than a good time. Research shows that listening to stories results in better listening skills, as well as improved attention span and imagination. It doesn't hurt language acquisition a bit either. Stories allow children a private world in which to make their own pictures, something which is in short supply in our culture.

There is no mystery about why it works. Long before a literate society began linking learning to books, good teachers were using stories as lessons. Sometimes the lessons were cautionary ones, like *Little Red Riding Hood*; sometimes they were about heros and heroines, like King Arthur. But they were always instructive.

School-age caregivers lead lives packed with activities. It may seem onerous to add even one more thing, no matter how valuable. But this is an easy one. You already have the tools necessary to become a storyteller; it only remains for you to apply them. Storytelling is an elastic art form, it expands and contracts to fit each teller. There are those who will only tell a few, and those who will make it an important part of life. Most of the world's tales have been told for so long that they practically tell themselves. All you need is a little patience and a little time.

You have a wealth of stories already. You know the old favorites: *Goldilocks and the Three Bears, Rumpelstiltskin*…that kind. Oh, you may need to refresh your memory a bit, but you will quickly recall them. So use what you have and tell what you know. Don't worry about the kids knowing the story already. They will in many cases. But the familiar, the known, has a particular appeal, and knowing the outcome can be the most fun of all. Many picture books are based on old stories, and make good ones to tell. *Caps for Sale* is one good example. Of course, stories are not limited to the picture book crowd. Older youngsters need them too. You would be dismayed by the number of children who have little knowledge of the stories we take for granted. So tell those classic tales. For the more mature kids, look for stories with adventure or suspense.

Many a good story can come from your own life; kids love to hear about the "olden days," or the time *you* got in trouble at school. Try to recall some personal or school events that might entertain. How about the time the snake got lost? Of course, you can always rely on your imagination, perhaps the best tool, to create a tale out of thin air.

As you see, there is plenty from which to choose. Now all you have to do is learn some. Remember that storytelling is a folk art form. Storytellers rarely memorize. It doesn't seem to suit most stories anyhow. Most of us tend to learn new skills a little at a time, with lots of slipping up along the way. Try to get acquainted with your story. (Of course, you have only picked a story that you *like*.) Read it aloud several times. Concentrate on the plot…what happens when. When you have that straight, concentrate on the people in the story, until they are familiar. Now check the story for special rhymes, words, or turns of phrase that appeal. You will want to remember them. Put the book down as soon as you can and tell the story to someone in your own words, preferably the kids. You may feel a little strange without a book. That's normal and it will pass. You can ease your discomfort and your listeners by confessing that this is a new experience for you. Soon you will be telling with comfort and confidence.

Once there are a few stories you enjoy telling, you can integrate storytelling into your program. Don't be in a hurry.

✪ **Prepare** the kids before starting a regular storytime by talking about it.

✪ **Set aside** a special time and symbol. Some providers have a candle which signals stories; others use a musical cue.

✪ **Choose** the time of day carefully. Children who are tired or hungry are not at their best.

✪ **Treat** these first experiences as if they were spinach. One bite is enough at first, so don't plan a whole program of stories right away. Your prudence will pay off, for soon you will be able to tell stories for longer than you thought possible.

✪ **Here is the hardest part of all:**

Don't ask your listeners if they learned something. This is not homework.

Trust the story and your telling of it. Let the kids take from it what they need.

With a little bit of luck, and application, stories will quickly seem a natural part of your program. You will find so many uses for them. If you are planning a visit to an observatory, you may recall an appropriate star story. When Christmas or Hannukah rolls around, there is always a story that seems to fit. Of course, Halloween is a natural. But mostly, you will tell for pleasure. The pleasure of hearing those compelling stories and seeing their effect upon the children. Then you will be glad that you expended the effort as you reap the benefits of this ancient and timeless art.

(Gay Ducey is a professional storyteller in Berkeley CA.)

(July/August 1987)

ACTIVITIES: PLANNING FOOD EXPERIENCES IN SUMMER PROGRAMS

by Bonnie Johnson

Essential to summer programs for school-age children are well-planned nutritious meals and snacks. Energy expended playing kickball, tag, bike riding, etc. requires nutritious food. Studies have indicated relationships between a nutritious breakfast and behaviors such as attention span and concentration. To enjoy summer programs children (and staff) need food that helps them perform at top level, that helps them control unwanted behaviors and helps them feel good.

The nutritional part of your program can be geared to the developmental needs of school-age children. School-age children can participate in all or part of your nutrition program-from planning menus, to ordering and purchasing food supplies, to preparing and cooking meals, to serving and eating meals and cleaning up.

Participation in your nutrition program meets their developmental needs of rule boundness, decision-making, participating in processes that directly affect them, and in real life experiences.

Planning Menus

By giving school-age children "rules" or guidelines by which to plan meals, you will appeal to their rule boundness and at the same time increase their knowledge of what kind of foods make a meal nutritious and/or meet USDA guidelines. For example, "rules" for planning lunches are:

   ☻ Have a meat or protein source
   ☻ Bread or bread sources (such as macaroni)

✪ Fruit or vegetable
✪ Milk

Have each child or groups of 2 or 3 children be responsible for planning one or more lunches. A good way to start is to plan one meal together. This is a good time to introduce why we eat certain foods. Be sure to have sample menus, cookbooks, recipes or other resources to help the children in this task. Small programs may easily accommodate all meals being planned by children; where larger programs may only be able to allow planning for snacks or breakfast or special meals.

Ordering and Purchasing Food Supplies

Participating in ordering supplies to match the menu plans provides useful math experiences: How many dozen eggs do we need to make scrambled eggs for 50 people on Monday and egg salad sandwiches on Thursday? And how much will it cost? Also problem-solving and decision-making levels: Should we buy the 10 lb. bag of flour at $2.50 or the 20 lb. bag at $4.25?

Purchasing Supplies

Educational field trips to local stores, farmer's markets, local farmers, and food wholesale distributors to purchase food items can provide experiences in comparative pricing, checking quality and quantities of different foods, as well as comparisons of different stores. If your program has food items delivered to your facility, one or two children could help check for receipt of all goods ordered, and for quality of goods.

Preparing Meals

From washing and peeling carrots and potatoes to cutting up fruit for fruit salad, to frying chicken or making tuna fish casserole, school-age children enjoy cooking food. They can take turns assisting the cook in the kitchen, can prepare their own breakfast or snacks or maybe lunch once a week. Preparing meals in a small group (maximum of 3 children) is best. The rest of the children can be pursuing other activities. This works well as long as they learn their turn will be coming at another scheduled time. Children will become acquainted with cooking tools: blender, food processor, steamer, etc. and measuring utensils. This is an opportunity for getting a first hand acquaintance with the metric system: use measuring cups and spoons calibrated in standard and metric system.

Eating Meals: The Best Part!

Having participated in the processes leading up to the actual consumption of food, school-agers tend to enjoy their meals more and be willing to experiment with new food tastes.

Clean Up

Don't overlook this essential part! School-agers feel a sense of usefulness and independence cleaning up after themselves. Also, questions can be raised in relation to left-over food: Can it be used for part of the p.m. snack? Does anyone have a dog to give the food to? What about a compost pile for the garden? How can we plan better to reduce the amount of left-over food?

Activities Related to Food

1. **Prepare and Eat A Meal from Another Culture:** Start with a culture related to one of your children. If you choose Mexican foods:
   - ❂ visit a Mexican restaurant
   - ❂ locate Mexico on a world map
   - ❂ invite a parent to tell about their life in Mexico
   - ❂ look up information about Mexico
   - ❂ make a piñata and have a Mexican party
   - ❂ learn how to make cornmeal from corn

2. **Make your own cookbook with children's and staff's favorite recipes:** Have the book printed and sell to raise money. Collecting and writing recipes, layout, drawing pictures, naming the cookbook are all parts of this project the children will enjoy. A visit to a local printer to investigate having the cookbook printed will provide information about printing as a career option as well as what the printing process is all about.

3. **Go on a "Sugar Hunt":** This works well after a discussion of the effects of sugar on teeth and body. (Use films and books from the library.) Have the children bring in cereal boxes, candy wrappers, vegetable cans, pre-packaged food wrappers, etc. Make lists of foods containing sugar as their first ingredient, second ingredient and foods with no sugar. (Remember school-age children love to make lists) They can even make a chart of the number of foods in each category, i.e. sugar as first or second ingredient and those with no sugar. A trip to the store or using the food boxes or containers brought from home to "play store" with are two ways to structure this.

(May/June 1981)

ACTIVITIES: MAKING PROJECTS SUCCESSFUL

by Eileen Cross

Often child care workers apologize to the school-agers when a planned activity is not successful. This negative attitude causes frustrations and stress for the adults and contributes little to the self-esteem of the kids. Frequently the school-agers end up believing they are the reason the project failed. To consider a project successful only when the outcome of the children's efforts are all the same is unrealistic. Nor is a project successful if the adult needs to finish it for that "perfect" look or to make corrections to achieve the "objective" of the project. The "successful" project is then done by the adult, not by the children. The adult then becomes solely responsible for the project. Frustration and stress for the adult and the kids and an unsuccessful project is the awful outcome.

What makes a successful project? Is there a magic formula for a successful project? No, there is no magic formula, but some helpful hints follow.

Plan Ahead

Planning ahead is a major component for a successful project. Will the project meet the needs of the school-agers? What materials will be needed for the project? Are the directions clear, yet not too simplified for the age level of the kids? Are *you* comfortable doing this particular project? For example: If you hate to cook, then don't try to do complicated cooking projects with the kids. You will be uncomfortable and so will they.

The day before you plan to do the project, review your plans. Are the materials ready and available to use? Nothing is as frustrating to a kid as waiting his turn to use the glue or waiting while the adult finds another pair of scissors. This is the point at which behavior problems—squabbling, whining, grabbing, fidgeting, interfering with other kids' work—may develop. This places unneeded stress on the adult and can lead to an unsuccessful project.

Allow Creative Freedom

Allow school-agers freedom to create their own end product, not your preconceived idea of how it should look or be. Therefore, the children not only have choice in doing one of several activities, but also choice in how to do a particular project.

Example: For a holiday activity, one project was to make stained glass hearts. Each child uses a heart-shaped cookie cutter for a mold and three pieces of hard candy for the "glass." The choice of colors was up to each child. Some chose red, others green, yellow, etc. The hearts were then baked at 350° until the candies melted. The different colors chosen reflected each child's unique creativity. The resulting project depended on the kids' choices and efforts, not the adults'. It was successful because the children did the project themselves (with a little help!) and because *they* were satisfied with the results.

Observe & Evaluate

Observe a project in progress. Be with the kids and do the project with them (but not for them!). Your involvement makes it possible for them to express their creative ideas. Encourage them to make suggestions for the current project as well as future ones.

Ask yourself the following questions:
- ❂ Are the children involved with the project?
- ❂ Through their creativity, do they stretch the ideas of the project?
- ❂ Are their skills being fairly challenged?
- ❂ Are the kids stretching or restricting their talents?
- ❂ Do they show interest through verbal communications and interaction?

Evaluate the answers to those questions for planning future projects.

(May 1988)

ACTIVITIES:
GOIN' ON A SNAKE HUNT

by Gaila Savery

Editor's Note: *The experience described here is an activity that can occur any time of the year, especially summer.*

I'd like to share one of my favorite ways to spend wonderful Oregon afternoons outside. The equipment you need is minimal: energetic children, your five senses, trust, respect, a first aid kit and a camera (optional). These elements and any outdoor environment can lead to one of the most fun and fulfilling activities you can share with your children—a SNAKE HUNT! Yes, I said "Snake Hunt." (Original idea thanks to Steve Musson.)

A trusting and respectful environment needs to be in place in order to do really successful, exciting things with children—like Snake Hunts!

One of the most important aspects to the actual Snake Hunt is the preparation that must be done ahead of time. From the very first day of the school year, we have spent many hours—both in discussions and in actions—reinforcing the concepts of **trust** and **respect**. The children have had a big impact on our definitions of trust and respect, and how it looks and feels to be trusted and respected. We as adults have consciously modeled behaviors that reflected these values at all times. You cannot build a trustful and respectful environment without giving that trust and respect to those you deal with—kids, coworkers, parents, others—on a daily basis. We must be able to communicate our needs, expectations and feelings openly and honestly in order to build trust and respect. These things take time and a lot of work. A trusting and respectful environment needs to be in place in order to do really successful, exciting things with children—like Snake Hunts!

Supportive environment in place, the announcement of an impending Snake Hunt generates excitement, questions, and planning sessions. "Where will we look?" "What will we see? hear? smell?" "How do we show respect to nature and its inhabitants?" What are the boundaries–are there any?" And the most important question: "What will we do if we find a snake?" (My biggest fear!) The children come up with most of the guidelines. I have only a couple: 1) I can see them and they can see me at all times; 2) We practice trust and respect. My personal goal is to observe and participate with children in their natural environment, out of doors. Preparation complete, we can set out on a Snake Hunt.

With that background in mind, I'd like to tell you the story of a Snake Hunt I participated in last fall. It's become one of my, and the children's, favorite "Remember whens." The school–Pleasant Valley Elementary, a country school (but any school would work). The setting–the walking path around the school grounds. The 16 explorers–15 children ages 5-10, and me. Four of the kids–Michael, Carl, Justin, and Leah–profess knowledge of the terrain and the hunt. They are my field guides and Snake Hunters Extraordinaire.

Feelings of freedom, discovery, trust and respect are being experienced by all of us.

The sun is shining, the fall air holds both warmth and chilliness. We can smell leaves and smoke from woodstoves. The afternoon that looms ahead is full of anticipation and excitement. We are ready to set out with our first aid kit, collection bags, and enthusiasm.

The children are eager and extremely excited about the possibility of seeing, hearing and/or touching a real live snake. We take the south path toward the creek. Going through the open field, eyes are focused downwards to any holes or dirt spots in the grass, because "you know that's where snakes hide." Carl is quite clear on this point.

As we continue we enter a grove of oak trees. The path winds in and around the trees, a whole new environment to look at and think about. Leah points out that the grass is gone and snakes could climb trees. Eyes and ears are really darting about now. Someone notices the rustling noise we make moving through the dry leaves and wonders if that would scare the snakes. "Could we step on any?" This thought is not very appealing to many of the hunters.

The children are now spread out up and down the trail, probably about 15-30 yards in front and behind me. They are very careful not to be out of sight around the bends in the trail. They are just as careful not to climb too high in the trees so I can't see them. We have only covered about 100 yards, and haven't seen any snakes. (Yeah! relief!)

Feelings of freedom, discovery, trust and respect are being experienced by all of us. It's difficult to put into words but is so visible on everyone's face. On with the hunt…

We come to a downed cedar tree, another good hiding place for "all kinds of bugs and snakes," says Michael. The texture of the tree and the way it peels it very interesting to the girls. "Could we use it to braid a rope or something?" "Why not? Let's try."

Snakes slither and slide in tall grass. "Maybe that's what we need to do to see them," says a kindergartener. "Let's try."

We clear the grove of trees and are faced with a huge field of semi-tall grass, old blackberry vines and just plain open spaces for running and exploring. Running out across the field, the boys stop dead in their tracks, turn around and look at me as though to say, "OK, we'll come back." They realize that we can see each other and it's OK to be about 100 yards away. Trust and respect–what a powerful combination!

Snakes slither and slide in tall grass. "Maybe that's what we need to do to see them," says a kindergartener. "Let's try." What a picture we are, all laying on our stomachs trying to slither. But, alas, no snakes. (Yeah!)

We continue on the trail winding around the field, seeing horses, cows, and sheep–and smelling them too. Now we are coming to different trees–evergreens– and another discussion on the smells, feels, and uses of these trees. Under the evergreens are nice beds of pine needles. "Crunchy," "soft," "pointy," "brown and red" are just a few of the descriptive words we use.

Our serious hunter, Justin, is now laying on his stomach because he saw a snake here at recess when he was in first grade (he's in fourth now). Well, he's right–a real sighting. Word spreads fast and loud–all 16 of us trying to see this poor, scared-to-death snake. "I'll touch it if you'll touch it." "No, I'm not going to." "Is it a baby?" "It's a yellow racer; they're the fastest you know." "Where'd it go?" "There it is!" The excitement, exhilaration and some fear are awesome. Their faces are all lit up and animated. This goes on for about 3-4 minutes, then the frightened snake finds an escape route. Disappointment quickly replaces all the excitement and exhilaration. The discussion of feelings (ours and the snake's) continues as we wander on.

Next is the duck pond, with some Canadian geese today. "Those are the kind of birds my uncle shoots." Now there's a moral discussion topic if I ever heard one. As we continue on around the playground, disappointment is evident in the slow pace and drooping faces. We accomplished the children's goal of finding a snake. But school is now in sight and we all know the hunt is coming to an end. No one wants this to happen.

The children felt as though they were in control of their own destiny. We worked together, shared, trusted, and respected each other.

However, the downcast faces and slow pace are quickly replaced with the thrill of sighting–yes!–another snake! (Two in one day. How could I be so lucky?) This is a full grown red racer that takes off instantly when it senses the children's excitement. The energy level is high now. The discussion and stories are beginning– I liken them to "fishermen" stories. "It was so big!" "I saw it first!" "Gaila wouldn't touch it!" "The girls all screamed!" and so on.

Well another 15 yards and we're back to the school. But there's one last great adventure for children of any age. The leaves from the huge old maple trees are in some average-size piles that are calling us. Guess what we answered! What a perfect ending to a spiritual, intellectual and emotional Snake Hunt.

This hour and a half could never be replaced by a craft project, a science lesson, a movie, tape, or any other teaching device. The children felt as though they were in control of their own destiny. We worked together, shared, trusted, and respected each other. It was a time I will never forget, nor will the children. It is a time we enjoy "remembering when," and, most of all, an experience we can't wait to try again.

Gaila Savery is Regional Supervisor of the Vermont Hills Family Life Center in Lake Oswego OR and is the recent past president of the Oregon School-Age Coalition.

(June/July 1999)

SUMMER ACTIVITIES AND IDEAS

JUNE

Magical Math

Here is an amazing math trick that will baffle the children. Have each child perform the following on a piece of paper:

1. Choose a number between 6 & 9.
2. Subtract 5 from that number.
3. Multiply the answer by 3.
4. Multiply that answer by itself.
5. Add together the digits in the answer (e.g. 25=7).
6. Subtract 4 from the answer.
7. Multiply that number by 2.
8. Subtract 6.
9. Select the letter of the alphabet that corresonds with the answer (e.g. 1=A, 2=B, 3=C, etc.).
10. Write the name of a country that begins with that letter.
11. Write the second letter in the name of that country. Write the name of an animal whose name begins with that letter.
12. Write the color of this animal.

Each of the children will have a "gray elephant from Denmark" written on their paper. ⚘

American Sign Language

American Sign Language is a language used by deaf people throughout the United States. In sign language, the hands and arms are used to make gestures which replace spoken words. This allows hearing impaired people to "hear" with their eyes.

Invite someone from a local hearing clinic or school for deaf children to the program to demonstrate sign language. In some areas there may be a drama group of deaf actors who perform through signing. Have copies of the American Manual Alphabet available and encourage the children to learn how to spell out their names and other words using this special alphabet. They can practice with friends or in front of a mirror. ⚘

Quick Change

Partners stand face to face and study each other for a few moments. Then each turns around and makes a "quick change," for example, untying a shoe lace, removing a hair ribbon, or tucking in a shirt. When partners face each other again they must try to guess what their partner has changed. To make the game more difficult increase the number of quick changes each time.

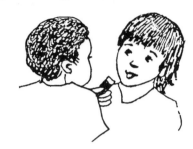

Under Cover Leader

Organize a group into a circle. A child is chosen as "it" and instructed to leave the room. A leader is chosen to direct the group in a series of motions, such as tapping the head, stroking the chin, slapping the thighs, pulling the ear, etc. The leader is to strive very hard not to be caught as the beginner of the motion. "It" has three guesses to locate the leader when she returns. If the leader gets caught, the leader becomes "it." ⚘

Mirror Images

Materials needed:
White paper (2 sheets)
White or colored chalk
Black crayon

Cover one whole sheet of white paper with the chalk. Cover the chalk with a heavy layer of black crayon. Place the other piece of white paper on top of the black crayoned paper. Draw a simple picture outline with a dull pencil. Press hard. Shade some areas. Turn the top paper over. You should have two pictures, one the mirror image of the other.

Tie-Dyed Papertowels

Materials needed:
Food coloring
Water
Bowls
Papertowels

Mix different colors of food coloring in separate bowls with water. Children fold the papertowels in unique ways, then dip the corners of the folded towels into the bowls of diluted food coloring. Carefully unfold and hang them up to dry. ⚘

Blob Tag

Blob is a tag game in which the blob continues to grow in size. The object is to be on the run and not to be eaten by the blob.

Define the boundaries before beginning. Anyone who goes outside the boundaries must join the blob.

One person is chosen to be "it" and begins chasing players and trying to tag them. When a person is tagged, she is absorbed by the blob, meaning she joins hands with "it" and continues to chase and tag others. When the blob grows in size to 4 players, the blob can split into two blobs of 2 people each. Play then continues until all players have been absorbed. The last to be absorbed is the winner and starts the next game. ⚘

Fairy Treats

To make fairy gifts to place in trees (see p. 115), spread graham crackers with peanut butter and birdseed. If fairies don't get them, who else will benefit?

	Monday	Tuesday	Wednesday	Thursday	Friday
JUNE HAPPENINGS	June 5–*World Environment Day.* Brainstorm a list of things kids can do to keep the earth clean and safe.	June 10, 1928 – Birthday of children's books author and illustrator, Maurice Sendak. Read his book, *Where the Wild Things Are.*	June 14 – *Flag Day (US).* Wear clothing that is red, white, and blue or printed with stars and stripes. Take a group photo of everyone in their patriotic garb.	June 21 – First day of summer. Celebrate by making your own popsicles. Fill ice cube trays with orange juice or fruit punch, insert toothpicks and freeze.	Father's Day is the second Sunday in June. Write a note to Dad telling him why you are lucky to have him for a father. Grandpas and uncles would love a letter too!
FUN IN THE SUN	Play "Duck, Duck, Splash." This is played like "Duck, Duck, Goose," but rather than being chosen as goose, you are splashed with a large, wet sponge!	June 18 is *International Picnic Day.* Celebrate by eating snack or having lunch in picnic style outdoors.	Take a nature hike to see how many different kinds of birds, trees and flowers you can identify.	Have a water balloon toss.	Collect insects in empty plastic jars. Then draw pictures and try to name all of the insects collected. Be sure to set the insects free at the end of the day.
USE YOUR SENSES	While blindfolded taste and try to identify different foods. Graham, saltine, and Ritz crackers work well.	<u>Also</u> while blindfolded see if you can tell the difference between pennies, nickels, dimes, and quarters by feeling them.	*Still blindfolded,* use your sense of smell to identify odors. Vinegar, soap, and cheese are good to use.	Blindfolded <u>once again</u>, see if you can identify people just by listening to their voices.	Learn to finger spell your name using the American Manual Alphabet (see p. 114).
MAKE BELIEVE	Sit on carpet squares and pretend you're taking a magic carpet ride. Float through the clouds to far away lands. What does the world look like beneath you?	Pretend you are a mermaid or a merman. Draw a picture of your ocean world. What would you look like? Where would you sleep?	Make gifts for elves and fairies and leave in branches of trees. See page 114 for a fairy gift idea.	Read aloud a chapter each day from *The Fairy Rebel* by Lynne Reid Banks.	Go on a fairy search. Look around brush, trees, long grass, and mushrooms. Keep your eyes open…the "little people" move quickly!
SALT & PEPPER	Mix up salt and pepper in a cup. Pour some water into the cup. Can you guess which will float to the top? (It's the salt.)	Color salt with colored chalk and layer the different colors in empty baby food jars.	Make salt dough for modeling. Mix 2/3 c. of salt, 1/2 c. flour, and 1/3 c. water. After sculpting, air dry or bake in 350 degree oven until hard.	Fill a glass with water and ice cubes. Wait a few minutes. Place a string on the ice cubes. Sprinkle salt on the cubes. After a few seconds pull the string. What happens?	Pop two batches of popcorn. Sprinkle salt on one batch, leave the other batch unsalted. Conduct a taste test to determine which batch is more popular.
POTPOURRI	Build marshmallow sculptures using toothpicks and marshmallows.	Sort through a pile of coins. Find the oldest, newest, shiniest, and most worn. Place coins under paper and make coin rubbings with crayons.	Spread shaving cream on a table and "finger paint" in it.	Relay – Put on a pair of thick winter gloves and unwrap a stick of chewing gum. Pass the gloves on to the team member next in line.	Sing a song in a "round."

Family Day

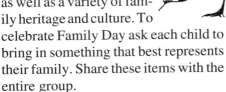

June 6th is Family Day. Children come from a variety of family structures, as well as a variety of family heritage and culture. To celebrate Family Day ask each child to bring in something that best represents their family. Share these items with the entire group.

Or, draw pictures or make collages that describe the children's families. ✍

Don't Forget Dad!

On the Friday before Father's Day have a luncheon for the adult males in your children's lives. Besides fathers, they could invite grandfathers, older brothers, stepfathers, uncles — any adult male who figures prominently in their lives. During the luncheon, let the children take turns reading a one or two line statement about why their father figure is important to them. ✍

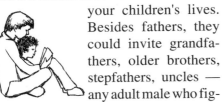

Money Faces

Martha Washington, the first First Lady of the United States, was born on June 2, 1732. Mrs. Washington was also the first woman to have her pictures on U.S. paper currency. In 1886, a one dollar silver certificate was issued and in 1902 an eight-cent stamp was also issued with her portrait.

Create a sample of paper currency or a coin leaving a place for children's portraits. Children can either draw in their self-portraits or bring in photos to use. Make sure the currency has huge values, just like the value we see in the children! ✍

A Day at the Beach

June is beach weather so plan a day at the beach for building sandcastles. So you don't live near an ocean beach? Look for lake areas with sandy beaches. Or create a beach in the program. If you have existing sand play areas in the program yard, divide the children into teams of 4-5 for a sandcastle building contest. Or use a watertable or large plastic dishpans filled with sand to create an indoor "beach." Let each child build a mini-castle, using the caps off shampoo bottles or hairspray containers for their "buckets." ✍

Note: If going to a real beach, remember your sunscreen and hats!

Salad Day

June 4, 1070 is the day recognized for the invention of Roquefort (commonly known as blue cheese) dressing. Celebrate by making healthful, delicious salads for lunch. Ask each child to bring in one item for either a garden salad or fruit salad (or combine elements of both!). The more variety in the salads the better—include different types of nuts, sunflower seeds, beans, broken up chips, etc. What different types of green vegetables can you find? How many different colors can you include in your salad? What is the strangest or most tropical fruit you can include? Also include a variety of light dressings, preferably fat-free. ✍

Wild Things

Children's author Maurice Sendak was born on June 10, 1928. Read *Where the Wild Things Are*. Let the school-agers dramatize the story. Don't forget to have a wild rumpus. Children can also draw pictures of their own "Wild Things." Find out what other books Sendak wrote for children. ✍

Fashionably Red

Fashion designer Bill Blass was born on June 22, 1922. Whenever anyone needed an idea on what to wear, he would advise "Wear something red."

Have a "Red and Wild Day" with everyone in the program wearing something red. Have a fashion show and look for inventiveness and originality in the children's red garb. Staff people should have a fashion show as well!

Let the children try their hands at designing clothes using paper cutouts or fabric scraps. ✍

Tree Rubbings

For a World Environment Day (June 5) nature activity, have the school-agers study the various trees at a local park. Have them do a tree rubbing by laying a white sheet of paper against the tree bark and rubbing the entire area of paper with crayon, chalk, or charcoal crayons. Press firmly in order to get the pattern of the bark on the paper. Let the children identify the trees they've rubbed through field guides, and compare the different bark patterns.

What other nature items can the children do a rubbing of? ✍

Ice Cream Goodies

What's a summer day without ice cream? June 15, 1854 the first ice cream factory opened. Bring in an ice cream maker and make homemade ice cream. Survey the children to find out their favorite flavors. Make a graph to show the results. Most popular flavor is the one that gets made. ✍

	Monday	Tuesday	Wednesday	Thursday	Friday
JUNE DAYS	June 5–*World Environment Day.* Create litter patrols and go to a local park to pick up trash (but no needles or glass!).	June 9– *Senior Citizens Day.* Visit a local retirement center. Take table favors made by the children to brighten up the seniors' lunch table.	June 18–*International Picnic Day.* Head to a local park with a picnic lunch and plenty of outdoor games. A rainy day? Spread cloths on the floor and picnic inside!	June 26–The Pied Piper of Hamelin was followed by 135 kids. Why? Find other Pied Piper stories. Re-enact the story with a parade through the program and outside.	June 30– In 1859 Jean Gravelet crossed Niagara Falls on a tightrope. Have a tightrope contest with a length of rope or thin piece of lumber lying on the ground.
SPECIAL JUNE EVENTS	June is **National Dairy Month**. Quiz children on dairy products. How many can they name? Trick question: Are eggs a dairy product?	June 9th is **Donald Duck's birthday**. Create your own cartoon characters. Hang a large piece of paper on the wall for children to create a cartoon mural.	The first week in June is **National Safe Boating Week**. Visit a local boat shop or marina for a tour. Find out about boat safety laws in your state.	June 14 is **Flag Day**. "Flag" comes from the old English word *fleogan* which means "fly in the wind." Make paper replicas of flags from your state or country of origin.	June 30 is **Halfway Day** because it's halfway through the year. How many days are left in the year? Have a "half" day–have lunch at half past noon with sandwich halves, etc.
VACATIONS	Take your program on a vacation. Visit a local travel agency for brochures on places the schoolagers would like to go. Select one or more places as a theme.	Plan a budget for your vacation. How will you get there? Where will you eat? What sites do you want to see? Put a $ amount to each item and add up.	Make a list of what you need to take on vacation. Make a suitcase from a cardboard box to pack your things. Use real items or draw their pictures or cut from magazines.	Plan an event to go along with one of the places you will visit. For example: a luau, a casino night, tea party, outdoor hike, swimming party, etc.	Make a vacation bulletin board and have children bring in photos or brochures from their family vacations. Provide time for those who would like to share their trip.
WEDDINGS	June is a popular month for weddings. Plan a mock wedding or wedding reception for the program. (Note: Be sensitive to different family structures and non-traditional relationships in the children's lives.)	Have more than one bride and groom, dressed in gowns and jackets. Let "guests" come up with creative and perhaps outrageous wedding attire.	Create a wedding reception hall by decorating with balloons, streamers, paper chains, etc. Cover tables with paper cloths; add a centerpiece.	At the "reception" serve cake and punch; hors d'oeuvres of cheese and grapes skewered with pretzel sticks. Let the children create a tiered wedding "cake" with decorated stacked boxes.	Find out about wedding customs from other cultures. Let children whose parents may have married in another culture bring in wedding photos to share.
NATURE LOVERS	Place a wire ring made from a coathanger on a section of grass and record what can be seen through a magnifying glass.	Go for a walk in the woods. Collect bird feathers, interesting shaped pebbles and rocks, do tree rubbings.	Decorate your rocks with paint or markers. Find creative ways to turn them into people or animals. Any one for a pet rock?	With the feather you find, cut the quill tip at an angle and make a slit for ink. Dip in ink and try writing with it.	Plant a flower or vegetable garden to tend during the summer. Or pick a spot to plant a tree sapling for future generations to enjoy.
BEACHY GOOD FUN	Go to a beach or shoreline of any body of water, even a stream or river. See how many interesting things you can collect from the area.	Create an ocean mural. Hang a large piece of blue paper on the wall. Decorate with sand, plants, brightly-colored fish and shells, all made from paper.	Serve a seafood snack. (Check for allergies!) Serve tuna, salmon, or sardines on bread or crackers. Take a fieldtrip to a local grocery to visit the seafood counter.	Cut out a shape of a sandcastle from cardboard. Smear the board with glue and shake sand over entire area. Add shells and other items for decorations.	Have a beach party! Spread beach blankets and towels on the floor, have picnic foods, tall cool drinks, play beach music and beach volleyball. Wear swim suits/beach clothes.

School-Age News Broadcast

Decide on roles and assignments for a school-age news broadcast. **Set designers** design the "set" or area where the news anchors who read the news will sit. **Reporters** collect newsworthy information from others in your school-age setting and write a brief report of each news item. **News anchors** read the news when they are directed to by the **News Director**. Don't forget to have a **marketing staff** who plan the commercials that appear throughout the broadcast. You'll also need **camera operators** to construct cameras they can use during the broadcast. Try using a large cereal or soap box with a small plastic or paper cup for the lens. It can be mounted on a stand and add wheels if you can. Produce the news broadcast for others in the program. ᘛ

Flag Flying

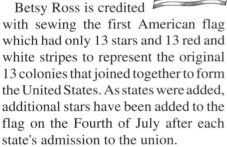

Betsy Ross is credited with sewing the first American flag which had only 13 stars and 13 red and white stripes to represent the original 13 colonies that joined together to form the United States. As states were added, additional stars have been added to the flag on the Fourth of July after each state's admission to the union.

If you were asked to design the American flag, what colors would you use? What symbols? Use colored construction paper and design your own flag. On the back write what the symbols and colors mean to you and why you chose them. ᘛ

State Birthdays

Kentucky, Tennessee, West Viriginia, and Arkansas all celebrate a day in June when they became states. Kentucky became the 15th state on June 1, 1792, and on the same date in 1796, Tennessee became the 16th state. Arkansas became the 25th state on June 12, 1836. West Virginia became the 35th state on June 20, 1863.

Find the date of your state's admission to the U.S. and plan how you would celebrate a centennial, sesquicentennial, or bicentennial anniversary of that date. ᘛ

Patently Inventive

Many inventors have created useful products that have made our lives easier. For example, Henry Ford completed work on his first car in Detroit on June 4, 1896. He started Ford Motor Company on June 16, 1904 and helped change how Americans would travel for years to come.

The U.S. Patent Office keeps track of inventions that have been created over the years. Registering their new product with this office protects the inventor from someone else using his (or her) idea without permission.

Other new products patented in June: June 8, 1869 - Ives McGaffey patented the *vacuum cleaner*.
June 23, 1846 - Antoine Joseph Sax patented the *saxophone*.
June 23, 1868 - Christopher Lathem Sholes patented the *typewriter*.
June 25, 1867 - Lucien Smith patented *barbed wire*.

Find facts about invention patents in addition to these and create a matching game by writing the dates, inventors, and inventions on separate cards for school-agers to match correctly. ᘛ

Famous Quotes

All of the people listed below have a birthday in June. Reproduce the list of names and list of quotes on paper for school-agers to match the right quote with the right person:
1. Frank Lloyd Wright (June 8)- an American architect who had global impact.
2. Anne Frank (June 12)- a Jewish teenager who hid in an attic from the Nazis for two years during World War II.
3. Wilma Rudolph (June 23)- an African-American track star who won three gold medals at the 1960 Olympics.
4. William Butler Yeats (June 13) - an Irish author and poet.
5. Helen Keller (June 27)- a lecturer, author and activist who was blind and deaf.

Quotes:
a. "Education is not the filling of a pail, but the lighting of a fire."
b. "When the sun is shining I can do anything, no mountain is too high, no trouble too difficult to overcome."
c. "Many persons have a wrong idea of what constitutes true happiness. It is not attained through self-gratification but through fidelity to a worthy purpose."
d. "Television is chewing gum for the eyes."
e. "I shall persevere in spite of everything, and find my own way through it all, and swallow my tears."
Answers: 1. d; 2. e; 3. b; 4. a; 5. c.

Things to think about and discuss:

What do you think about the quote in (a) above? Where do you get an education? Do you receive education anywhere other than school? Make a list of all the places where you might become more educated. What other comparisons could you use to describe education? Draw one of them around your list.

Think about the quotes from Helen Keller, Anne Frank and Wilma Rudolph. These women never knew each other. Based on their quotes, make a list of three qualities or traits that they seem to share. Think of yourself having these same traits and draw a picture of what you could be doing. ᘛ

	Monday	Tuesday	Wednesday	Thursday	Friday
JUNE DAYS	June is Zoo Month. Make a miniature zoo with animal cracker animals and "natural" habitats.	June 14 is Flag Day. It honors the day in 1777 when the Continental Congress adopted the first offical American flag. Find a picture of that flag.	Four states have birthdays during the months of June (see page 118). Design a birthday balloon or banner for each.	Donald Duck's 65th birthday is June 9. Garfield the Cat began on June 19, 1978. How old is he? Draw a cartoon to introduce these characters to each other.	Design a Father's Day card for your father, stepfather, grandfather, uncle, or other male role model.
SUMMER DAYS	June 17 is the first of the year's longest days and shortest nights. These extended days last through June 26. Find out how long each day is during this time.	Summer begins on June 21. Draw a mural that shows what activities everyone would like to do during this summer season.	Plan a fantasy summer vacation. Where would you go? Make a scrapbook of pictures from your dream summer vacation.	Brainstorm a list of all the things that you would like to do during your summer program. Be creative and make the list as long as possible.	Let everyone vote for 3 things from the list they most want to do during this summer. Count the votes to get a Top Ten list of things to do.
CRAZY ABOUT CATS	June is Adopt-a-Cat Month. Ask those who have adopted a cat to tell about their experience.	Make a chart to represent how many in your group have pets and the types and numbers of pets they own. How many have a cat in their home?	Conduct research (through books or the computer) to learn about the different breeds of cats. Make a model of a cat using clay or other art media.	Invite a veterinarian or someone from a pet store to talk to the group about different types of cats and how to care for them.	Ask an animal control officer or someone from an animal shelter to talk about their programs and the laws that protect cats. Make a poster to promote cat welfare.
FRISBEE® FRENZY	The first Frisbees® were manufactured on June 4, 1957. How old would the very first Frisbees® be?	Try out as many games as you can that you can play with a Frisbee®. How about Frisbee® baseball?	Brainstorm with the group and come up with a list of other creative uses for a Frisbee®, other than as a toy.	Throw a Frisbee® as far as you can every day for one week. Make a chart to measure your progress. Were you able to increase your distance?	Try to keep a Frisbee® in the air (without touching it!) as long as possible. Use a watch with a second hand to measure how long the Frisbee® remains in flight.
DEMOCRACY	On June 2, 1924, the U.S. Congress granted citizenship to all American Indians. Pretend you were an Indian then, and express how you feel about this. Why?	On June 6, 1872, Susan B. Anthony, an early women's rights advocate, was fined for trying to vote. Make up and perform a skit dramatizing an attempt to vote.	Juneteenth is celebrated on June 19 to honor the day in 1865 when the slaves in Texas were set free. Read a book about the Underground Railroad.	The legal voting age was lowered from 21 to 18 on June 30, 1971. Take a poll in your school-age program to find out what age people should be able to vote. Why?	Find out what you must do in order to vote in your state. Ask your parents or another adult about when they voted for the first time.
PATENTS	Charles Goodyear patented his process for vulcanizing rubber on June 15, 1844. What can you make of 5 or fewer components, one being a rubber band?	William Clarkson, Jr. patented the bicycle on June 26, 1918. Decorate bicycles for a celebration parade.	Be inventive. Think about what product might make life easier now. Draw a picture or write a description and show how useful it could be.	Become an inventor! Create your own new product using modeling clay and toothpicks or straws, or recycled "junk."	Write a letter as if you were requesting a patent on your new product. Include why you think your product is useful.

Poet's Workshop

In honor of William Butler Yeats and all poets, encourage the school-agers to try their hand at poetry. Here are a few ideas to inspire them:

● Use an overhead projector to project different colored tissue paper on the wall. Ask the children to call out words that describe the colors. You might need to suggest a few words to prompt them. For example, if the color is yellow, you might think of "sunny," "happy," or "pale." Combine the words to create a group poem.

● Offer sensory experiences, such as letting the children touch sticky dough, smell oregano, hear the sound of a bell in their ears. Work together to list words describing these sensations.

● Listen to classical, jazz or blues music. How does the music make the children feel? Write these feelings on paper.

● Look at familiar things from a different perspective: crawl around on the ground, turn items upside down and describe what you find, or look at common, everyday items close up through a magnifying glass. How did your perspective change? Write down these perceptions. ♻

Kick Volleyball

A new twist on an old game, where players use feet and knees instead of hands to play volleyball.

Set up a low net by hammering two stakes into the ground about 7 feet apart. Tie a rope between the stakes.

Divide players into two teams. The teams line up on either side of the net and try to kick the ball back and forth over the net. Players count aloud each time the ball goes over the net. If players touch the ball with their hands or if it rolls away from the playing area the counting must begin all over again. Try to set a record for the number of times the ball goes over the net. ♻

What If?

This is a fun game to pass the time while you are waiting in line, riding on a bus or just relaxing.

Ask the school-agers to describe what the world would be like if:

● dinosaurs still ruled the Earth
● electricity had never been invented
● all gravity suddenly disappeared

Use your imagination and invent more scenarios. ♻

Hit the Spot

Put a coin, button or any other round object on the ground. This is the "spot." Give each player an index card with his or her name written on it. One at a time the players are blindfolded and try to set their card on the spot.

For added challenge, try spinning the players around three times before sending them off to find the spot.

Use this game as an opportunity to increase measuring skills. After the game measure how far each person's card is from the spot. Don't focus on winning and losing, instead make it a group challenge to guess the correct measurements. ♻

Home-Made Sidewalk Chalk

Ingredients:
✔ 4-5 eggshells
✔ 1 teaspoon flour
✔ 1 teaspoon very hot water
✔ food coloring

Wash and dry the eggshells. Put them into a bowl and grind into a powder. Put flour and hot water into another bowl. Add 1 tablespoon of the eggshell powder and a few drops of food coloring, Mix well.

Shape this mixture into a chalk stick. Roll the stick up tightly in a paper towel and let it dry for three days. ♻

Spray Bottle Art

Style #1

Draw with washable markers on a large sheet of glossy fingerprint paper. Try to color all over the paper. Take the drawing outside and hang it up on a fence.

Fill a spray bottle with water (use a plant sprayer or other spray bottle, well washed out). Aim the bottle at the drawing and squirt, trying to get all parts of the paper wet. The water will cause the colors to run down, creating interesting new patterns and shades.

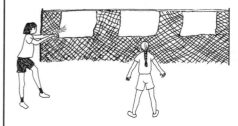

Style #2

Fill three spray bottles 3/4 full with water. Add tempera paint to each bottle, one red, one yellow and one blue. Cap tightly and shake to mix the water and paint. Hang a large sheet of paper outside on a fence. Spray the paint at the paper. Try mixing colors. ♻

Father's Day

In honor of Father's Day, invite the fathers or other male mentors in the children's lives (uncles, grandfathers, Big Brother) to the program for career day. Let these male role models describe what they do for a living. Consider starting a "Big Brother" program for those children who have no positive male mentors in their lives. ♻

	Monday	Tuesday	Wednesday	Thursday	Friday
JUNE BIRTHDAYS	June 12–birthday of Lou Gehrig, a famous baseball player. He died of ALS. Research this disease to find out what's being done to end it. Play a baseball game in Gehrig's memory.	June 13–birthday of poet William Butler Yeats. Try writing some poetry. See page 120 for tips on inspiring young poets.	June 14–birthday of Burl Ives, a folk singer from the 50s and 60s. Have a singalong of his song "I Know an Old Lady" (who swallowed a fly). Illustrate the different verses.	June 29–birthday of author Antoine de Saint-Exupery. He wrote *The Little Prince*. Read the story aloud. Talk about the hidden meaning of the story.	June 30–birthday of Lena Horne, a famous jazz and blues singer. Listen to her music. How do her songs make you feel? Happy? Sad?
PAPER CLIPS	Build a bridge using only drinking straws and paper clips. Have contests to determine whose bridge is longest, highest, strongest.	How many paper clips will it take to sink a styrofoam meat tray in a tub or sink of water? Write down all guesses, then try it out.	Cut out paper fish and attach a paper clip to each. Tie a magnet onto a string and "catch" the fish with the magnet. Try it while blindfolded for an extra challenge.	Link paper clips together to make necklaces, bracelets or crowns. Think of other innovative ways to wear paper clips and have a fashion show.	Use a magnet to make sculptures with a pile of paper clips.
BEAN BAG GAMES	Make your own bean bags by filling an old sock with dried beans or small beads. Tie the open end of the sock securely with yarn or sew it.	Bean Bag Tic-Tac-Toe: Make a large tic-tac-toe board on the floor with masking tape. Players toss bean bags onto the square, trying to get three in a row.	Move in different ways while carrying a bean bag on your head. Try walking, jumping, dancing.	Clean two plastic milk jugs and cut them in half horizontally. Use the handled portions of the jugs as bean bag catchers. Toss the bean bags back and forth with a friend.	Draw your own targets on paper. Assign points for each target area. Tape the target to a wall and toss the bean bag at it. Try to score points.
PLASTIC BOTTLES	Collect plastic 20 oz. or 2-liter bottles. Ask families for donations of their clean, empty bottles.	*Bottle Bowling*: Fill ten bottles half full of sand. Cap the bottles tightly. Roll a ball toward the bottles and try to knock them down.	*Wave Bottles*: Fill a bottle half full with water. Add food color and glitter if desired. Add baby oil to fill the bottle completely. Cap tightly and tip over.	Practice blowing into clear, empty bottles to make a noise. Have a bottle band. For best effect, use bottles of different sizes for different notes.	*Bottle Fountains*: Poke holes into a plastic bottle with a nail. Take outdoors and fill with water. Great for water play on a hot June day.
ONE CENT	How many drops of water can a penny hold? Make your prediction, then use an eye dropper to add one drop at a time until the water runs off.	*Pitching Pennies*: Stand two feet from a wall. Toss a penny as close to the wall as you can without hitting the wall. See who can get the closest.	*Penny Walk*: Take a walk around your neighborhood. Every time you come to a corner, flip a penny. Heads, you turn left; tails, you turn right.	What can you buy for a penny? Take a field trip to a store to find out.	Invite every family to send in a small bag of pennies. Count the pennies and donate the money to a charity, such as the ALS Foundation (see box on Lou Gehrig).
BEAT THE HEAT	Cool off with a lemonade stand. Stir up a pitcher of fresh squeezed lemonade and sell glassfuls to parents or other customers.	Make paper fans. Accordion-fold paper and glue on decorative jewel or glitter. Use the fans to keep cool on hot days.	Fill dish tubs with cool water and ice cubes. Experiment with measuring cups, plastic tubes, food coloring and different-sized containers.	Relax under a shade tree. Bring a book to read, sketch on a drawing pad or just practice doing nothing.	Have a beach party! Bring the beach to the program. Put on tropical music, lounge on beach blankets, serve fruity drinks, put on your shades and relax!

PLAN YOUR JUNE ACTIVITIES!

THEMES:

_____

_____

_____

_____

STAFF PERSON

_____

_____

_____

_____

ACTIVITIES:

_____

_____

_____

_____

_____

_____

_____

_____

FIELD TRIPS:

_____

_____

_____

_____

_____

_____

SUMMER ACTIVITIES AND IDEAS

JULY

Patriotic July Celebrations

Let's Have A Parade!

Plan a Fourth of July parade. Have children use old clothing and art supplies to create costumes representing an important person, place, thing, or idea related to the country's independence. Take your parade to a nearby nursing home, hospital or preschool child care.

Patriotic Poets

Provide samples of poetry from an assortment of children's books. List the following words on a chart or chalkboard:

independence	parade
July 4th	firecracker
flag	freedom
sparkler	holiday
red, white, blue	nation
country	fireworks

Have the children use any of these words (or others that they come up with) to create patriotic poems.

Patriotic Murals

Plan and paint a mural depicting the signing of the Declaratoin of Independence, a Fourth of July parade, a fireworks show, or a summer picnic with friends. To create a fireworks effect on the mural, children can dip plastic drinking straws into tempera paints and gently blow the paint onto the paper (being careful not to suck in on the straw!).

Patriotic Presentations

In small groups have the children write a story and plan how they will act it out for the others. Give them a few ideas for their creative scripts, such as:

The little firecracker that lost his blast…
The first Fourth of July parade…
The invisible Fourth of July celebration… ᚛

Flag Flying

Think of all the ways that an American flag may be flown or displayed. Where do you usually see an American flag? How many different ways can you think of? Some possibilities include:

> from a flag pole
> from a building
> at half mast
> with other flags
> in a parade
> behind a speaker
> on a casket

Flag Factory

American flags are made by many different manufacturers. They may be made out of cloth, plastic, paper, or other materials. Plan for and set up your own American flag factory. Give your flag factory a name and make a sign. Design a floor plan for the factory. Set up the factory area using existing furniture and large appliance boxes. Decide which employees are needed for the factory and give them job titles. "Hire" employees for these jobs. Design the process for making flags, using colored construction or butcher paper. Will each flag be made entirely by one worker or will flags be made in an assembly-line fashion? Write an advertisement to "sell" the flags your factory produces. What price will you charge for your flags? ᚛

July Birthdays

Below are famous people with birthdays in July. How many names do the children recognize? Do they know what these people are famous for? Create a matching game on a large chart or on individual papers and see how many the children match correctly with their occupations or achievements:

July 4 - **Stephen Foster**, a Southern composer known for "Camptown Races" and "Oh, Susannah."

July 12 - **Bill Cosby**, comedian and television star.

July 20 - **Sir Edmund Hillary**, the first mountain climber to reach the peak of Mt. Everest.

July 21 - **Robin Williams**, a comic and movie star.

July 22 - **Emma Lazarus**, an American poet, who wrote "Give me your tired, your poor, your huddled masses yearning to breathe free…" inscribed on the Statue of Liberty. ᚛

We All Scream for Ice Cream!

Chocolate, Banana, Peanut Butter Shakes

Peel a banana and cut it into bite-size pieces. Freeze the pieces for several hours.

Mix the following ingredients together in a blender:

> 1 cup of chocolate ice cream
> frozen banana pieces
> 1/4 cup of creamy peanut butter
> 1 cup of milk

Enjoy your creamy cold chocolate, banana, and peanut butter treat!

Coffee Can Ice Cream

Use two coffee cans for each five (1/2 cup) servings you plan to make. Clean regular (1 lb.) and large (2 1/2 lbs.) coffee cans with plastic lids work best.

Mix the following ingredients in the smaller coffee can:

> **1 pint of cream or Half-and-Half**
> **1/2 C. sugar   1 tsp. vanilla**

Place the lid on the can. Put about one inch of crushed ice in the bottom of the large can and cover it with one tablespoon of rock salt. Place the small can on top of the layer of ice and salt. Pack about 6 cups of ice around the remaining space in the large can, alternating layers of ice and rock salt (about 12 Tbsps.). When filled, put the lid on the large can. Roll the can back and forth on a flat, hard surface for 10 to 15 minutes. Remove the smaller can and take off the lid. If the ice cream is too soft, repack the cans with fresh ice and salt and roll the can a few minutes longer until the ice cream becomes firmer. ᚛

	Monday	Tuesday	Wednesday	Thursday	Friday
SOMETHING TO CELEBRATE	July is *National Peach Month, National Hot Dog Month*, and *National Baked Bean Month*. Honor each of these foods at lunch or snack.	July is *National Parks and Recreation Month*. Plan a trip to a nearby park or gather materials about a national park and plan a fantasy vacaton.	July is *Anti-Boredom Month*. Make a list of all the things you want to do in July to fight off the "Boredom Blues."	July is *National Picnic Month*. Make a picnic lunch to serve outdoors. Go to a nearby park or simply spread blankets in a shady spot near the program.	July is the beginning of the "Dog Days" of summer. These are the hottest days of the year. Imagine all the different ways you can cool off. Be creative!
I SCREAM FOR ICE CREAM!	July is *National Ice Cream Month*. National Ice Cream Day or "Sundae Sunday" is the third Sunday in July. Celebrate one day later with "Sundae Monday."	The ice cream cone was invented on July 23, 1904 in St. Louis, MO. Make your own Coffee Can Ice Cream (see p. 124) and serve in cones.	List as many different flavors of ice cream as you can. Make up a few exciting names for imaginary flavors. What would you include in these new flavors?	Make and enjoy Chocolate, Banana, Peanut Butter Shakes (see p. 124).	On July 8, 1881, a Wisconsin pharmacist, Edward Berner, invented the ice cream sundae. What would you use to create a perfect ice cream sundae for yourself?
WHEN FREEDOM RINGS	July 4, 1776 – The Continental Congress passed the Declaration of Independence, creating the United States. How old is the U.S. today? Have a birthday party to celebrate.	July 14, 1789 – Bastille Day is celebrated every July 14th in France. What event led to this holiday? How is it like our July 4th celebrations?	July 4, 1826 – John Adams and Thomas Jefferson both died on the 50th anniversary of U.S. independence. What was each man's contribution to the fight for freedom?	July 1, 1867 – Canada Day is celebrated on this date when Canada became a self-governing dominion. Decorate the room with red and white for Canada's flag.	July 4, 1884 – France presented the Statue of Liberty to the United States as a 100th birthday present. What does the Statue of Liberty represent?
POSTAL NEWS	On July 26, 1775, Ben Franklin became the first Postmaster General. What was his job? If you were the Postmaster, what changes in the mail system would you make?	The first U.S. postal stamps with glue on the back were issued on July 1, 1847. Draw a design of your own postage stamp.	Start a stamp collection. Children can collect stamps from mail received at home and at the program. How many different types of stamps can you collect?	Write letters to children who are sick and in a local hospital.	Set up a "mail" system and encourage children to write to each other. Have a mail drop with children taking turns being "Postmaster" and delivering the mail.
AROUND THE WORLD	Amelia Earhart was born on July 24, 1898. Find a book about this pioneer aviatrix who disappeared during an around-the-world flight. Trace her flight on a map.	On July 2, 1937, Earhart's plane vanished over the Pacific Ocean while in flight. Draw a mural depicting what she would have seen on her flight before disappearing.	On July 22, 1933, Wiley Post completed the first solo, around-the-world air voyage in 7 days, 18 hours, and 49 minutes. How many minutes was he in flight?	In *Around the World in Eighty Days* by Jules Verne, read about an exciting hot air balloon race to see who could go around the world first.	Plan your own trip around the world. Get brochures from a travel agency and plan where you would go and what you would do on your trip.
IN OUTER SPACE	NASA was created on July 29, 1968. What does "NASA" stand for? How many sites for developing, launching, and tracking space flights does NASA have?	On July 15, 1965, the "Mariner IV" satellite transmitted the first close-up photos of Mars. If you lived on mars what would you look like? Draw a Martian self-portrait.	John Glenn, Jr.'s birthday is July 18th. He was the first American to orbit the earth in a space ship. Draw a picture of what he saw from space.	Space Week is observed July 20-26 to celebrate when Neil Armstrong became the first man to walk on the moon on July 20, 1969. What did he say during that historic occasion?	Cosmonaut Svetlana Savitskaya became the first woman to walk in space on July 25, 1984. Practice your own space walk. What would your movements be like?

Create a Writing Workshop

Words Within Words

Write a short story on chart paper. Post the story for an afternoon or several days and let children circle or underline all the words that they find within other words. Example:

My mo<u>ther</u> likes to e<u>at</u> choco<u>late</u> c<u>ake</u>. <u>Yester</u>d<u>ay</u> I <u>baked</u> <u>one</u> <u>for</u> <u>her</u>. <u>She</u> <u>said</u> <u>that</u> it w<u>as</u> yum<u>my</u>!

Writing Center

Create an area where children may express themselves freely in writing. Surround the area with print, including magazines, catalogs, labels, and samples of the children's stories and poems. Provide children with books, dictionaries, word cards, and alphabet charts. Set out trays or baskets of different types of paper (lined, blank, colored, card stock, etc.). Offer statio-nery with envelopes, note pads, sticky notes, computer paper, adhesive labels, folders and clip-boards. Give children a variety of pens, pencils, crayons, and markers. Furnish staplers, tape, rulers, and scissors so that children may create their own books. ✂

Mask-Making Tips

Use a paper sack, paper plate, posterboard, or large cereal box for your mask. Add features using construction paper, yarn, string, foil, markers, and crayons. Attach with glue, staples, or tape.

To make cones for noses or horns, cut out a circle. Cut a slit from the edge of the circle to the center. Overlap the edges and glue or tape together. For a taller cone, cut a pie-shaped wedge from the circle. To attach the cone to your mask, cut a circle in the mask a little smaller than the large end of the cone. Push the cone, point first, through the hole. Make five slits in the wide end of the cone. Bend back the tabs created by cutting the slits and tape them to the inside of the mask.

To curl paper for eyelashes, hair and mustaches, cut strips of paper. Curl the strips by wrapping them tightly around a pencil, marker, or broom handle.

To keep your posterboard or paper plate mask in place, hold the mask up to your face. Make a dot where the mask touches your ears. Put a paper reinforce-ment over each dot. Poke a hole in the center of each reinforcement. Attach strings to the holes to tie the mask onto your head. Be sure to cut large eye holes in your mask so that you can see well when wearing your mask. ✂

Boxy Boxes

Animal Boxes

Create animals using small cardboard boxes for the animals' bodies. Paint the boxes or cover them with colored paper. Draw and cut out the animals' body parts from cardboard, construction paper, or other boxes. Try making a lion from a gelatin box, an alligator from a tooth-paste box, and an elephant from a frozen vegetable box.

Box Puppets

Hand Puppet: Stand a small cereal box, gelatin box, or pudding box on a small end. Draw a horizontal line all around the center of the box. Cut the box on the line along three sides, leaving one of the wide sides of the box uncut. Fold the box in half on the line that was not cut. Decorate the box puppet. Put your fingers in the top of the box and your thumb in the bottom of the puppet. Move your fingers to make the puppet "talk."

Stick Puppet: Punch a hole in the bottom of a small box. Insert a straw in the hole. Tape it firmly. Decorate the stick puppet.

You can use a clean fast food box as a stick puppet and decorate the inside of the box for the puppet's mouth.

Box Buildings

Use milk cartons, small cereal boxes, gelatin or pudding boxes, and other small boxes. Paint or cover the boxes with colored paper. Use construction paper for roofs, doors, awnings, windows, and chimneys. Cut window and doors out if desired. A rectangle of posterboard can be folded in the middle to form a peaked roof or cut a semi-circle from paper and curl it up to form a wide cone, gluing or taping the ends together. ✂

Answers for U.S. Presidential Families (see page 127)

1. Lucy Baines Johnson Turpin is the daugh-ter of President Lyndon Johnson.
2. The last 10 U.S. Presidents and their terms of office are:

Harry Truman	1945-1953
Dwight (Ike) Eisenhower	1953-1961
John F. Kennedy	1961-1963
Lyndon B. Johnson	1963-1969
Richard Nixon	1969-1974
Gerald Ford	1974-1977
Jimmy Carter	1977-1981
Ronald Reagan	1981-1989
George Bush	1989-1993
Bill Clinton	1993-present

3. Julie Nixon Eisenhower is the daughter of President Richard Nixon.
4. The current U.S. President is Bill Clinton. He lives in the White House with First Lady Hillary Clinton and Chelsea Clinton, who attends college in California.
5. Nancy Reagan is the wife of President Ronald Reagan.
6. *Millie's Book* is the book that President George Bush's dog, Millie, "dictated" to First Lady Barbara Bush.
7. Rose Fitzgerald Kennedy was the mother of President John F. Kennedy.
8. See the list of presidents and their terms in office (above).
9. Jacqueline Kennedy Onassis was the widow of President John F. Kennedy. ✂

JULY IDEAS CORNER

	Monday	Tuesday	Wednesday	Thursday	Friday
NATIONAL HOLIDAYS	Canada Day is July 1, celebrating when Canada became self-governing. Find a picture of the Canadian flag. Make your own Canadian flag with construction paper.	The U.S. celebrates Independence Day on July 4. Like those founding fathers, write a declaration of independence for your own new country.	Create a name for your new country. What holidays would you celebrate? Write or draw a depiction of the new national holiday you would create.	Design a flag for your new country. What colors would you select and what would they represent? Make a flag for your new country.	Bastille Day on July 14 is France's independence day. Find out why that day is important in French history.
WRITING WORKSHOP	Become a daily news writer. Write "Daily News" on chart paper. Let everyone add to the chart each day with news they would like to share.	Beatrix Potter was born on July 6, 1866. She was an English children's writer and wrote *Peter Rabbit*. What other characters did she create?	Find words within words. Write a story and then mark all the words you can find within other words. (see page 4)	Clement Clark Moore was born July 15. He wrote "Twas the Night Before Christmas." Write a poem beginning "Twas the night before vacation", or July 4, or camp, etc.	Write a rebus story on a large sheet of paper. Use pictures cut from magazines and catalogues to substitute for some of the words. Take turns reading each other's stories.
FUNNY WOMEN	Phyllis Diller was born on July 17, 1917. She was a housewife who turned comedian. Can you think of other housewives who became comedians? (e.g. Roseanne)	Think of the funniest person you know. How do they use humor? Can being funny be an asset? How? How is humor sometimes used inappropriately?	Estelle Getty was born on July 24, 1924. She is a comic actress who played on the TV show "Golden Girls." Become a comic actor. Write a funny skit and act it out with a few friends.	Gracie Allen, born July 26, was wife and comedy partner of George Burns. She was his "straight man" by pretending not to understand his jokes. Tell jokes with a partner. Take turns being the "straight man".	What is the funniest thing that has ever happened to you? Start a Comedy Club with your friends. Collect and share jokes and riddles with each other.
MASK MAKING	Make an animal mask. Act as if you are that animal. Can your friends guess who you are? (See page 126 for mask-making tips.)	Write a play and make a mask for each character. Act out the play for your friends by yourself, changing masks when you change characters.	Make a mask of each member of your family. Act out each of your family members working at some household chore.	Make a mask of yourself. Trade masks with a friend and pretend that you are each the other person.	Make a mask to show what you would like to become: an astronaut, a chef, a teacher, etc. Wear the mask and act as if you were that person.
BOXY BOXES	Collect as many small boxes as you can. Stack your boxes as high as you can. How many boxes would it take to be as tall as you are or to reach the ceiling?	Make an animal from a small box adding cardboard or construction paper legs, head, and tail. (See page 126 for ideas.)	Make hand puppets and stick puppets from small boxes. (See page 126.)	Construct a city of box buildings, houses, castles, and businesses.	Use small boxes to make vehicles for your city. You might make trains, cars, buses, boats, planes, and helicopters from small boxes.
PRESIDENTIAL FAMILIES	1.) Lucy Baines Johnson Turpin was born on July 2. Which U.S. President was her father? 2) List the last 10 U.S. Presidents. (All answers on page 126.)	3.) Julie Nixon Eisenhower's birthday is July 5. Which U.S. President was her father? 4.) Name the current U.S. President and his family members.	5.) Nancy Reagan was born on July 6. Which U.S. President is her husband? 6.) What presidential pet wrote an autobiography with the First Lady's help?	7.) Rose Fitzgerald Kennedy's birthday was July 22. Which U.S. President was her son? 8.) How many U.S. presidents have there been in your lifetime?	9.) Jackie Kennedy Onassis was born on July 28. Which U.S. President was her husband? 10.) Would you want to be related to the President of the U.S.? Why or why not?

Wacky Olympics

Celebrate summer with a fun and silly Olympics competition. Some ideas for games:

● Potato Sack Race
● Water Balloon Toss
● Pie Eating Contest: use small bowls filled with whipped cream for pies…no hands!
● "Dizzy Dash": spin each contestant around five times and race for the finish line.
● "Flipper Waddle": each contestant wears swimming flippers then races for the finish line.

Come up with your own ideas to add to this list. Present medals or ribbons for both winner and wackiest finish (number of times falling, etc.). 🚲

Field Trip Activity Box

Make your field trip bus rides more fun for everyone by packing a field trip box.

Use a sturdy plastic box or milk crate to put in supplies like books, paper on clipboards, pencils, markers or crayons, string (for Cat's Cradle games), travel games (decks of cards, trivia games, etc.) and information about your destination. Use empty plastic peanut butter jars with lids to keep small objects like pencils or crayons in one place. See page 129 for more bus activity ideas. 🚲

DJ for a Day

In the May issue creating a school-age television news broadcast was suggested. Now how about a radio show?

Meet with the group to decide what type of radio station the school-agers want to develop and make up a name for the station. Choose one or two of the kids to be broadcasters and choose radio personality names.

All radio stations have news broadcasts, so some children can write short news stories about events that are happening at the school-age program. You'll also need some commercials to read between songs. Kids can make up silly advertising jingles for their favorite products.

Invite children to bring in tapes or CDs of their favorite songs to play on their radio show. (You may want to check their selections for appropriate lyrics before playing them.)

When the show is ready, the kids can record the broadcast on a blank cassette tape using a tape recorder. When they're finished recording they can rewind the tape and play it back for everyone to hear.

Make this an ongoing summer project so all of the children who wish to have a turn at being broadcasters can have a chance.

As an extension of this project, either before or after you have your own broadcast, try to arrange a field trip to a local radio station to see how one really operates. Or invite a local radio personality on a popular station to visit the program. 🚲

Cloud Watching

On a cool morning, have the children lie on their backs outside and watch the clouds move through the sky. Give each child a sketch pad and pencil to draw what they see. Encourage them also to write down their observations of the cloud formations. Collect the observations and drawings for a display everyone can enjoy. 🚲

Millennium

Play a game in which each child in turn says "I'm preparing to enter the next millennium and I'm taking with me…" As this phrase makes its way around the circle, each player repeats all the items already proposed and adds one of her own.

A variation on this game can be "I'm on my way to the next millennium, but I'm leaving behind…" (wars, famine, etc.) See page 129 for more millennium activities. 🚲

Recycling Crayons

We all have baskets of old broken crayons around, and it seems that many school-agers would rather use pens or markers to write with. Here are a few ideas to transform those old crayons into fresh new activities.

First, simply remove all the crayon wrappings and use an old cheese grater to shave the crayons.

● Sprinkle the crayon shavings onto construction paper and lay the paper in the sun. The colored crayon bits will melt into a beautiful new art creation.
● Spread crayon shavings between two pieces of waxed paper. Heat the waxed paper with a warm iron to melt the crayon. Trim the edges of the paper and hang in a window.
● Add other treasures (leaves, twigs, bits of fabric) to the waxed paper and make it into a colorful placemat. 🚲

	Monday	Tuesday	Wednesday	Thursday	Friday
JULY DAYS	On July 1 the U.S. Congress authorized the first postage stamp. Take a field trip to your local post office to see how mail is sorted and routed.	July 5, 1810 is the birthday of *P.T. Barnum*, creator of the Barnum & Bailey Circus. Hold your own circus, with clowns, gymnasts, "lion" tamers, etc.	July is *National Tennis Month*. Ask families to loan their tennis racquets and practice hitting balls against the wall. Or go to a public tennis court for real games.	July 7 is Japan's *Star Festival*. Children tie poems to bamboo sticks and offer them to the stars. Write your own poems to celebrate this day.	July 1 is *International Juggling Day*. Learn how to juggle bean bags, balls or handkerchiefs. Invite a juggler to the program for a demonstration.
SAND ART	Color sand by mixing in a bit of dry tempera paint. For lighter colors use salt instead of sand.	Use the colored sand to make interesting designs. Drip glue onto tagboard and sprinkle the sand onto the glue.	Sand bottles: Pour sand into a clear plastic bottle through a funnel. Layer different colors. Use a toothpick to shift the sand layers for a "wavy" look.	Add water to a bucket or sandbox full of sand. Create sand sculptures and have a sand museum.	Ask families to bring back samples of sand from their vacations. Create a display of the different types. Note where they're from and differences in color and texture.
YEARBOOK CLUB	Start a yearbook that will chronicle your program activities throughout the summer. Begin by asking kids to draw pictures of their favorite summer activities.	Get one or two disposable cameras. Give these to the children and encourage them to take photographs representing your summer activities.	Assign some children to be reporters for the yearbook. Have them interview other children and staff about the activities taking place.	Glue all of the stories and pictures onto white paper. Let the children trim the photos and decide on the order of the pages.	Make copies of the yearbook for everyone. Keep a color copy of the yearbook for the program.
MILLENNIUM	With sidewalk chalk, create a timeline in millennia. Show both B.C. and A.D.	Design a logo to commemorate the millennium. Use it for T-shirts or book covers.	Play a game at least a millennium old. For example: dominoes (3500 B.C.), marbles (2000 B.C.), or checkers (1000 B.C.).	Write a letter to the future. Tell about your life, food, games, tools, education, energy sources, etc. Write it for someone to read in the year 3000.	Illustrate your letter with as many pictures and newspaper clippings as you can, documenting prices, styles, and how things look.
BACKWARDS	Have a *Backwards Day*. Do everything the opposite of normal. Walk backwards; eat on the floor instead of tables. Reverse your entire daily routine.	*Mirror Writing*: Write a secret message by writing the letters and the word order of the sentence backwards. Hold it up to the mirror to see the message.	Tape paper to the underside of a table. Kids lie on their backs and draw pictures upside down.	Try saying the alphabet or something like the Pledge of Allegiance backwards.	Have a backward relay race. Walk backwards to the finish line. For a variation, walk backwards while carrying a ping pong ball on a spoon.
ARE WE THERE YET?	*Roadside Scavenger Hunt*: Before you leave on a trip, make a list of objects children might see out the window. Work together to find all of the items.	*Countdown*: Look for numbers that you can see from the window of the bus. Start with the number 100, then find 99, 98 and so on.	*1-1000*: Leader thinks of a number between one and one thousand. Children take turns guessing; leader says "higher" or "lower" to help them deduce the correct number.	*Spell It*: Write the letters of the alphabet on small pieces of paper. Put the letters into a hat. Players each choose five letters to try and make a word.	As a group watch for signs that provide a first line. Add a second line to make a rhymed couplet. For example: *Bridge may freeze... Drive slowly please.*

Stained Glass Art

Bring out the "Louis Tiffany" in your school-agers with this stained glass art project. Each child needs a glass or acrylic box or bottle (recycled from home), bottles of glass stain in various colors, paintbrush, and permanent black marker. The glass stain and brushes can be found at any art supply store or stores like Wal-Mart.

First draw a design on the bottle or box with the marker, making sure each section is large enough to apply paint in between the black lines. With the paintbrush apply one color of the glass stain to one or two sections on one side of the box (for bottles this isn't necessary, you can carefully turn bottle). Rinse out the brush with water, then apply a second color to a section or two. Continue with other colors until one side is complete. Let dry completely before working on the other side. When completed, encourage the children to sign their "masterpiece" on the bottom. They can give it as a gift or keep it as evidence of their artistic ability! ✿

Variation on a theme:
Sun Catchers!

"Stained glass" sun catchers are another fun art project using color. Each child will need: 12-inch lengths of black pipe cleaners, ribbon or cording, food coloring, plastic wrap, plastic or paper cups, and white all-purpose glue.

First plan the design: a heart, a flower, a hot air balloon, or some other simple shape. Then bend pipe cleaners into the desired shape and glue onto a section of plastic wrap. Glue small pieces of the pipe cleaners inside the design to add details, like the different sections of the hot air balloon's fabric. Let it dry.

To add color, pour 3-4 tablespoons of glue into a cup. Add 5-10 drops of food coloring and stir. Make a separate cup for each color needed. Pour colored glue into each section of pipe cleaner

shape, with a different color in each section according to the design.

Let project dry for a day. When dry, carefully peel away the plastic wrap. The colored glue will look translucent.

Attach ribbon or cord and hang the sun catchers in the window for all to admire. ✿

Supreme Justice

On July 2, 1908, Thurgood Marshall, the first African-American on the U.S. Supreme Court, was born in Baltimore, MD. He served for more than 20 years as the director-counsel of the NAACP Legal Defense and Education Fund. His greatest legal triumph as a lawyer occurred May 1, 1954 when the Supreme Court decision in Brown vs Board of Education declared an end to the "separate but equal" system of racial segregation in public schools. He served on the the Supreme Court from Oct. 2, 1967 until retiring in 1991.

In recognition of Marshall's contribution to justice, replicate the Supreme Court. Choose nine "justices" who will listen to a case and let them "weigh the merits" of the case. Also have lawyers, a defendant, a plaintiff, and courtoom spectators. Pick a problem, have both sides prepare and present their case, let the Supreme Court "hand down" a decision.

Did you know that on the Supreme Court, there doesn't have to be a unanimous decision? Often the individual justices disagree with the outcome of the case and decisions are made by a majority vote. Let your "School-Age Supreme Court" justices defend their individual opinions. ✿

Cool Down Corner

Add a splash of interest to your reading center. Bring in a small plastic swimming pool, some beach chairs, and a few beach towels. Fill the swimming pool with books, both the

program's and those favorites from home the children might want to share (make sure their names are in the books). The children will enjoy sitting in the beach chairs or lying on the towels as they soak up the good books.

Add a collection of sports titles such as *The Field Beyond the Outfield* by Mark Teague, *The Mud Flat Olympics* by James Stevenson, *Dulcie Dando Soccer Star* by Sue Stops, *A Boy Named Boomer* by Boomer Esiason, *Teammates* by Peter Golenback, and *Baseball ABC* by Florence Cassen Mayers

Stamps of the Future

The stamps shown above were the winning designs by children from ages 8-12 when they were asked what they thought the future would look like.

As a project for your stamp club or for all the school-agers in your program, have your own "What will the future look like?" drawing contest.

The U.S. Postal Service has all types of stamps that makes collecting fun for kids. They can get stamps featuring various insects, space exploration, desert life, under sea life, and more. Go to your local post office to get information on starting a club. ✿

	Monday	Tuesday	Wednesday	Thursday	Friday
INDEPENDENCE DAYS	On July 4, 1895, the poem *America the Beautiful* was published. It was later set to music. Rehearse the song as a choir and perform for parents.	Independence Day "Sparklers." Wrap 2" x 6" red, white and blue paper strips around paper towel tube and glue. Tape 1/2" shiny silver strips of wrapping paper to one end of tube.	July 1 is Canada Day when the Dominion of Canada was formed in 1867. Study each Canadian province. What is unique about each one?	What famous waterfall do the U.S. and Canada share? Who in the group has been there? Research stories about people who used to go over the falls in barrels.	July 7, 1898, Hawaii became a U.S. territory. When did it become state? Have a luau. Wear leis, drink tropical juices, eat pineapple, play Hawaiian music or pull out the ukeleles!
STAYIN' COOL!	July 3 – "Stay Out of the Sun Day." Play in the shade of a tree, in a tent, or inside to give your skin a rest from ultraviolet rays.	July 3-Aug. 15 - *Air Conditioning Appreciation Days!* How did people cope with summer heat before air conditioning? Name all the ways you can think of to stay cool.	Make a "pamaypay" (Filipino for fan) to stay cool. Decorate a 6" round or square piece of tag board. Use glue or staple gun to attach it to a 12" long wooden stick.	*Ice Cube Relay*: Players carry ice cubes in spoons to finish line and back, then transfer ice cubes to next players' spoons. Play outside and try to finish before ice melts.	*Ice Cream Pies*: Melt half gallon of any flavor ice cream. Stir until smooth, then pour into graham cracker pie shells. Refreeze. Cut into slices and serve with hot fudge.
CLOUDS	Lie on your back and watch the clouds float by. Let your imagination soar. What do you see? Can others see the shapes in the clouds you see?	Arrange and glue white cotton balls into an imaginary shape on construction paper. Draw and color the rest of the picture. Share with the group.	Imagine you are on a cloud looking down. What would everything below look like? Draw a "birds eye" view of your neighborhood.	Cloudland Canyon is the name of a park in north Georgia. What does that name suggest? Why do you think that name was given to the park?	Divide into teams. Give each a U.S. map. Teams search for and list on paper all of the place names with the word "cloud" in them. (Ex: St. Cloud MN).
JUST FOR FUN	July 5, 1910–P.T. Barnum's birthday. He created "The Greatest Show on Earth" circus. Have a mini-circus, with "lion" tamers, acrobats, clowns, and jugglers.	July 10–Arthur Ashe was born. He has a long list of firsts as an African-American tennis player, including 1975 Wimbledon champ. Practice hitting tennis balls against a wall.	July is *National Parks & Recreation Month*– Plan your own park. What would it have in it? Lots of play equipment? Animals? Hiking trails or obstacle course? Draw a picture.	*Water Play Day*– Bring in plant misters, squeeze bottles, and other water toys. Have water relays, ride bikes through the sprinkler, eat popsicles to "chill" completely.	Have a cookout to celebrate *National Hot Dog Month*, *National Baked Beans Month*, and *"July is for Blueberries" Month*!
CRAZY DAYS	*Favorite Color Day*– Everyone wears their favorite color. Maybe face paint in that color too. Take a survey of the "best" color based on how many are wearing same colors.	*Backwards Day*– Wear clothing backwards; reverse the day's activities; write backwards message on board for kids to decipher; eat dessert first, then lunch.	*Clash Day*–Everyone wears mismatched clothing. Have a contest for the most outrageous mismatched clothing.	*Chow-Down Day*– Everyone brings in healthful snacks from home. Let kids nibble throughout the day on fruit, veggies and dip, cheese and crackers, etc.	*Etch-A-Sketch Day*– July 12 is the 40th anniversary of the Etch-A-Sketch. Have several available for Etch-A-Sketch drawing contests.
RECYCLE IT	Use old restaurant menues to practice math skills. Kids total the items ordered, add tax, calculate tips, and give change.	Long ago a person's last name represented his livelihood. Look in old phone books to find names that show what profession that family may have been. (Example: Baker)	Let one child add together five phone numbers from a page in the old phone book. Circle those five and another five and ask another child to figure out which numbers were added.	Encourage technical reading skills. Have software guides, equipment instructions, VCR manuals, etc., for kids to read.	Use old travel brochures to practice reading, graphing, or map skills.

PLAN YOUR JULY ACTIVITIES!

THEMES: STAFF PERSON

_____   _____

_____   _____

_____   _____

_____   _____

ACTIVITIES:

_____   _____

_____   _____

_____   _____

_____   _____

_____   _____

_____   _____

FIELD TRIPS:

_____   _____

_____   _____

_____   _____

_____   _____

SUMMER ACTIVITIES AND IDEAS

AUGUST

Games of the Arctic

Children's toys of the Arctic were historically made from natural objects such as bone and ivory, animal skins and fur. Balls were often made of sealskin stuffed with fringed strips of hide.

A hunting strategy used to sight caribou or whales at some distance has evolved into a blanket toss game. A group of hunters form a circle holding a walrus hide with one hunter in the middle. When they pulled the hide tight, the hunter would be tossed high in the air to look for the caribou herd or whales.

You can try this game using a blanket and a ball. Stand a group around the blanket, all holding the edges, with the ball in the center. On signal from the leader, pull the blanket tight and see how far you can make the ball go in the air. Keep trying to beat your record.

Also for entertainment, children would play with Eskimo yo-yos, two balls hanging from string, twirled in the air. To make your own, cut a hole in each end of two tennis balls. Cut two lengths of string, one about four inches longer than the other. Pass the string through each ball. Knot the end to the keep the ball from pulling off. Tie the unknotted ends together. The object is to get the balls moving in opposite circles. The trick is to keep your hand moving up and down rather than around. Keep trying, it's lots of fun! ✧

A Trip Around the World

Plan a theme for the month celebrating the diverse world we live in. Let the children form small groups, each concentrating on a country of their choice. Try to encourage a representation from around the world. The groups create a flag and choose a game, crafts, music, dance, and a food dish to share about their country. They can research how some cultural traditions were created, like the information in the previous activity. They can also develop traditional costumes.

Have the group work on their plans one or two days a week to keep the project exciting. At the end of the month, invite parents to a vacation around the world. Have the children demonstrate the music and dances of the countries they studied, while displaying arts and crafts and serving the various foods. ✧

First Aid Kits

Have the children make and carry their own "mini" first aid kits when away from the program. Make these kits before your first field trip of the school year.

Take any rectangular box such as computer disk holders, band-aid containers, etc. and cover the outside with construction paper or contact paper and label with "First Aid" symbols. Fill the kit with band-aids and antiseptic wipes. Include each child's own emergency contact numbers: parents work numbers, and who to contact in case parents cannot be reached. Include any known allergies and other medical alert information, as well as change for pay phone calls. ✧

Waterscopes

Waterscopes are a fun way to view a pond full of interesting critters. Use a half-gallon milk carton, cutting off the top and bottom so you look into a square on the cut end. Tape the bottom edge so the carton won't tear the plastic. Cover the bottom and sides of the carton with the thickest clear plastic you can find. use a rubber band to hold the plastic while you tape it to the inside of the open end. When you find a good viewing pond, tilt the waterscope as you slip it into the water. This keeps air from being trapped between the plastic and the water. And be sure you don't get water in the open end. Take a field trip to your favorite pond and start exploring. ✧

Carnival M.A.S.H.

For your carnival fun (see page 135), set up a booth that resembles a M.A.S.H. unit. Ask a local clinic for old X-rays of broken bones, and make an X-ray machine from cardboard boxes. "Patients" can have an X-ray taken of their arm or leg, and out pops a real X-ray! Also have materials for making splints, cloth strips for bandages, and red food coloring for "blood."

School-agers thrive on the melodramatic and love to ham it up. They'll want to choose their wound (probably the gorier, the better!) and will delight in stumbling about the carnival site groaning over their supposed mishaps, or terrifying their unsuspecting parents. ✧

Kids in the Kitchen
Cool Fruit
Ingredients:

Round slices of banana, dipped in lemon juice; bite size pieces of cantaloupe, watermelon and honeydew melon; red or green seedless grapes.

Let the children prepare the fruits and spread them on a foil-covered baking sheet. Freeze for 3 hours. Enjoy! ✧

This cool summer treat is from the book Healthy Snacks.

Fantastic Photos

Remember all your SAC summer fun with photos. Let the children take five or more photos each, using disposable cameras. They can arrange the photos in an album and add their own narratives. Brightly colored paper cut into fun shapes and placed behind and around the photos make a memorable display. Keep the album close to the sign-out area so parents can take a peek. ✧

	Monday	Tuesday	Wednesday	Thursday	Friday
ALL ABOUT AUGUST	August 9 — *National Book Lovers Day.* Start reading a book aloud today - kids' choice.	August 1-7 — *International Clown Week.* Plan a carnival theme with balloon games, juggling and clown skits.	August 4-10 — *National Smile Week.* Face paint smiles on yourselves or each other and have a joke-telling contest.	August 8-10 — *Mosquito Awareness Week.* Find a book on insects to learn more about mosquitoes. In Alaska, some consider mosquitoes the state bird!	August 16 — *Watermelon Day.* Enjoy watermelon for snack. If eating outside, have a seed-spitting contest as children eat.
THEMES	*Time Travelers —* Build a time machine and travel to the days of dinosaurs. Papier maché your favorite dino and create a play.	*High Flyin' Adventure —* Make kites, paratroopers, or hot air balloons. Invite a pilot to speak to the kids about flying.	*Water Olympics —* Take advantage of the hot weather to get wet with water games such as water balloon toss, sprinkler relays, and squirt gun target practice.	*Dream Day* - On Aug. 28, 1963 Martin Luther King, Jr. gave his famous "I Have A Dream" speech. Present your dream in a skit or mural.	*Olden Days —* Howdy Pardner! Dress up as they did in the Old West and have a square dance.
CARNIVAL FUN	Use refrigerator boxes to create booths for various games like the bean bag toss game. Fill an empty soda can with pebbles or sand and knock it off a ledge with a tennis ball.	Other booths can include games like dropping clothes pins in a bottle, pin the tail on the donkey, and a hula hoop contest or demonstration. — — — Set up a "M.A.S.H." unit. (See p. 134.)	Another booth idea is to have a jar filled with jelly beans and participants have to guess how many are in the jar. Winner gets the jar of jelly beans.	Set up food booths serving light snacks like pretzels and nachos. — — — — Set up lawn games like ring toss.	Find ways for the kids to earn their tickets all month for spending at the carnival. Invite the parents too.
RAINY DAY DELIGHTS	**Story Bags** — Give each child or small group a bag with 5 random items inside. Ask them to create a drama to share with the others, using the items as props.	**Freeze Dance** — Play music and let the kids dance. Freeze each time the music stops. Play music fast and slow for added fun!	**Pitch a Tent** — Put up a tent inside or use blankets and rope for a make-shift fort. Create a group story by passing a flashlight. Use the flashlight for hand shadows too.	**What Was That?** Have children sit in a circle and pass small unknown objects behind their backs. Then they write down their guesses in order.	**Balloon Relay** — Two even teams pass balloons under their chins down the line. No hands! If it drops, start over.
BUTTONS	**Button Printing** — Press button on inkpad, then on paper. Use a pen or markers for finishing touches.	**Jewelry** — String buttons on heavy thread for a necklace or elastic cord for a bracelet. Get creative and make earrings too.	**Button Mosaic** — Draw a simple picture on paper and fill in with different sized and colored buttons.	**Button Face Magnets** — Paint a face on a button, cut felt in shape of a head around button and glue a magnet on the back.	**Button on a String**— String is tied to form a circle large enough for all the players to hold it overhanded with both hands. IT tries to guess who has the button as it passes hand to hand along the string.
JUST FOR FUN	*Physical Fun —* Plan organized games like soccer, basketball, and Ultimate Frisbee®. Play for fun - no eliminations.	Plan frequent cooking projects like Rice Krispies® treats and Jello® jigglers.	Use music as background sound during "hang-out" time, or create a wild event with a lip sync contest.	*Junior Leaders —* Have the older kids plan a watermelon treasure hunt for the younger kids and then share in the delicious rewards.	*Cartooning —* Find a book on cartoon basics and teach simple faces. Let the kids make their own cartoon strip.

Clowning Around

National Clown Week (first week in August) is a great time for some silly fun. Create a three-ring circus at your program with a clown act in one ring, jugglers in the second ring, and acrobats in the third. Paint clown faces and make paper clown hats, then have a clown parade. March around the playground or gym in clown garb playing music on coffee can drums, kazoos, or pots and pans.

Clown Face Paints

Supplies: cold cream, tempera paints, cotton swabs, small cups.

Put some cold cream in each small cup. Add a few drops of paint to the cold cream and stir, adding paint until you obtain desired colors. Use cotton swabs as paint brushes and use a new swab every time you change colors, and for each child. This paint goes on smooth, doesn't itch, and washes off easily.

Paper Clown Hats

Supplies: construction paper, stapler, glue, "decoratives."

To make these three-cornered hats, fold a rectangular piece of construction paper lengthwise about 1/2 inch up. Glue sequins, buttons, tissue paper scraps, etc. all over the hat. Or decorate with crayons, colored markers, or stickers. Bring together the top two corners in the back and staple. ✄

Group Games

Early August mornings, before the noon day sun really beings to blaze are the perfect times for playing field games. In addition to traditional favorites, try some of these games:

Human Pinball

Form a circle with everyone facing outward. Two or three children stay in the middle of the circle. The players forming the circle must throw a ball from between their legs, trying to hit someone in the middle. Once hit, they trade places.

The Great Chain

Form a big circle with everyone holding hands. Then, everyone face in one direction and tighten up as close to each other as possible. Next, have everyone sit down. If done correctly, they will all be sitting on each other's laps.

The Ha-Ha Game

Have the children lie on the ground (the floor if indoors) in such a way that each child has his head on the stomach of the person next to him. To start the game, the first child says "Ha." The next child says "Ha-Ha," the third says "Ha-Ha-Ha," and it continues with each person adding another "Ha." This game never fails to bring giggles galore! ✄

Memories

With the start of a new school year just around the corner, August is a good month for looking back and remembering the best moments of the school-age program, especially the fun theme days or field trips that took place during the summer. August is also a time to look ahead and wonder about the coming school year. Scrap books, time capsules, and predictions are three interesting activities that encourage children to think creatively about the past, present, and future.

Scrap Books

To make a scrap book, punch holes in 9" x 12" sheets of oak tag or heavy construction paper. Bind the pages together with colorful yarn or ribbon. Choose a title for your scrapbook, something as simple as "My Scrapbook" or as elaborate as "Mollie's Marvelous Memories." Decorate the cover with crayons, markers, stickers, glitter or whatever suits your personality. Then decide what you will put into your book. You may want your scrapbook to follow one theme all the way through, such as favorite art projects, or simply a collection of fun events, with photos of friends, postcards from field trips, or awards.

Time Capsules

A cardboard shoe box with a cover is all it takes to create a personal time capsule. The boxes may be decorated with tempera paints, colored contact paper, or gift wrap. The children should fill their time capsules with items that represent them as they are right now. Some suggestions are: recent photographs, height and weight, list of best friends, a sample of artwork or handwriting, a newspaper article from that day's paper, a tape recording of the child talking or singing.

After loading the time capsule, seal it tightly with string or masking tape to help resist the temptation of opening it too soon. Mark the outside of the time capsule with the child's name, the date it was sealed, and the date it is to be opened in the future.

Predictions

Making predictions about the future is fun! Predictions can be silly, serious, or a bit of both. It encourages children to think about their dreams and set goals for the future. Sometimes it helps children to get started if you provide them with some topics, such as school, family, friends, clothes, toys, then decide on a period of time. For instance, "At this time next year, my family will…(live in a different house, own another pet, etc.)." Older school-age children can work on this independently, but younger children may need to dictate their predictions to an adult or older child who writes them down. Put the predictions in a safe place waiting for that day in the future when you'll see which predictions came true!

	Monday	Tuesday	Wednesday	Thursday	Friday
AUGUST DAYS	The first week in August is *National Clown Week*. Let the children take turns creating funny clown faces on one another with face paints. (see page 136.)	Francis Scott Key was born on Aug. 1, 1779. He wrote the Star Spangled Banner, the U.S. national anthem. Find out the circumstances under which he wrote the song.	Make up a song that will be the official anthem for your school-age program. The lyrics should represent the values and characteristics of your program.	The first electric traffic lights were installed in Ohio on August 5, 1914. Play the traditional game, 1-2-3-redlight.	Imagine what our roads would be like today without traffic lights. Make up a story about the day all the traffic lights disappeared.
BOTTLES, JARS, & CARTONS	**Wave Bottle:** Fill a plastic soda bottle half full of water and 1/4 with vegetable oil. Add a few drops of blue food coloring. Cap tightly and rock gently to see wave motions.	**Bug Cage:** Cut holes or windows into the sides of a small milk carton. Put the carton inside a nylon stocking. Use a twist tie at the top to open and close the cage.	Prepare blue raspberry gelatin and pour into large glass baby food jars. Add Swedish fish candies and chill. A cool ocean treat for a hot August day.	**Ocean in a Jar:** Layer plain or colored beach sand in an empty pickle jar. Add small shells, sequins, etc. Fill slowly with water. Tightly screw on lid.	Glue a small lump of clay to the inside of a baby food jar lid. Arrange dry or silk flowers in the clay base. Screw the lid on carefully for a mini-floral arrangement.
WET AND WILD	Fill a basin with water and experiment to see which objects will sink and which will float.	Have a water balloon toss.	Fill a plastic soda bottle with water. Make a hole in the cap and screw on tightly. Squeeze the bottle and watch the water spray. A fun, safe way for water play.	Make a water slide with an old plastic tarp and a garden hose.	Buckets of water and big, clean sponges are fun for splashing around in the sun.
VINTAGE GAMES	"Vintage" games may be brand new to many children. Play with marbles, introduce jump rope rhymes, teach some yo-yo tricks.	Learn to play jacks.	Have a hula hoop tournament. How long can you keep the hoop spinning around your waist? What else can you play with a hula hoop?	Use sidewalk chalk to draw a hopscotch game on the black top.	In a ball field or grassy area, play Red Rover or Kick the Can.
GO CAMPING!	Sit around a make-believe campfire (or a real one if you have access) and sing songs or tell ghost stories.	Pretend you are away at a sleep over camp. Write a letter to your parents. Describe everything about camp–your counselor, the food, your favorite activities.	Take an "Upside Down Hike." Peek under rocks, leaves, and sticks to see what might be living underneath. Put things back the way your found them.	Attach magnetic tape to colorful constuction paper fish. Tie lengths of yarn to sticks and fasten a paper clip to the end of each string. Use an empty wading pool to fish in.	Sit quietly outdoors and bird watch. Have a bird book handy to help with identification. Borrow binoculars for close up observations.
WHAT NOW?	Rub a metal teaspoon in your hand until it's warm. Then tilt your head back slightly and place the bowl of the spoon on your nose, with the handle hanging down.	Have a 3-legged race.	Let the children build forts or tents using sheets, blankets, chairs, tables, or whatever equipment is available.	Learn to say the alphabet backwards.	Spread a blanket on the lawn and do some cloud gazing. What does each cloud look like?

Sleuthing

Have a spy day. Read a mystery. Play "I Spy." Have the group follow clues to find the snacks for the day. Use magnifying glasses to examine footprints the children have made in the sand or dirt. Determine which footprint belongs to whom. Write messages in invisible ink or secret code. Play "Hide and Seek." Find pictures, or live examples, of creatures that use camouflage to hide. Do word searches and "find the hidden picture" puzzles. Dress up in disguise. Draw a special spy tool, like Inspector Gadget's crazy machines. ⚙

Dream On

August 28 is *Dream Day*. Do you remember your dreams? Do you dream in color or black and white? If people are bilingual, what language do they dream in? Can you smell things in dreams?

Set aside some daydreaming time. Think about things that have happened or might happen or that you would like to have happen. Keep a journal about your daydreams and check in a few months to see what has "come true." ⚙

Dream Catchers

The Chippewa and other Native Americans make dream catchers out of a wood hoop with a web and feathers that hangs above the bed of a newborn baby or a newly married couple. The bad dreams get tangled in the web but the good dreams float through the web, down the feather, and onto the sleeping person in bed.

To make a dream catcher you'll need: 9" white paper plate, 12" of yarn, beads (store bought or hand made paper or clay beads), feather, masking tape, pencil, scissors and a hole punch.

Draw a large ring inside the rim of a paper plate. Cut out the center of the plate to the inner edge of the ring. Then, cut off the outside rim of the plate, leaving the ring. Punch about 16 holes around the ring. Wrap masking tape around one end of the yarn. Poke the taped end of the yarn into the top hole and pull through, leaving about 3" at the end. Create a web by crisscrossing  the yarn to fill up all the holes around the ring. Leave the center of the web open. End by bringing the taped end of the yarn back to the top hole and tying this to the other end. Cut a piece of yarn about 8" long. Loop it through the bottom hole and even the ends. Pass several beads up the yarn, and slip a feather into the beads. Knot the ends of the yarn. Hang the dream catcher over your bed. ⚙

(Original source: *The Kids' Multicultural Art Book* by Arthur Terzian, Williamson Publishing, 1993.)

Heat Conduction Experiment

Fill three cups with equal amounts of hot tap water. Place (handle side down) a metal knife in one cup, a plastic knife in another, and a wooden knife (or a piece of wood the approximate size and shape of a knife) in the third cup. Stick a pat of butter on the exposed (cutting) end of each knife. All three pats of butter must be the same size. Place a sugar cube on top of each pat of butter.

Ask the children to guess what will happen. Wait a while and watch. The material that lets heat move through it most easily and quickly is the best conductor. The butter on the best heat conductor will melt the fastest and the sugar cube will fall off. ⚙

(*With thanks to Bill Nye, the Science Guy.*)

Solar Bowls

Put two cups of water in each of three bowls that are the same size. Put a few drops of yellow, blue, green, and red food color in two of the bowls. The water should look black from the mixture of colors. Cover one of the bowls of dark water with a clear glass plate or clear Pyrex baking dish. The third bowl has plain water and no cover. Leave all three bowls in the sunshine for several hours. Test the temperature of the water in each bowl with your finger. Which is hottest? Why?

A solar panel makes energy by using the heat-absorbing power of black and the heat-trapping power of glass—like the covered bowl. ⚙

End of Summer Medals

Have an end of summer awards ceremony and give out medals to the children for various accomplishments, but make sure everyone gets one. The kids can make the medals and brainstorm on awards to be given. How about "Most Friendly," "Best Listener," "Most Joyful," "Most Helpful," or any others you can think of.

To make the medal, cut out a 3" diameter cardboard circle and cover it with foil. Use permanent marker to write in the type of award. Glue the end of a 3" piece of ribbon to the back. ⚙

	Monday	Tuesday	Wednesday	Thursday	Friday
SMILE!	August 1-7 is both *National Clown Week* and <u>National Smile Week</u>. Big smiles are catching. Wear one and see how many others you can infect.	Paint smiley faces on paper plates using yellow and black paint. Exhibit them in a "Happy Gallery."	Talk about the things that make you smile. Make a bar graph to show how many happy-making things others in the group share.	Cut apples into "smiles" (quarters). Spread with peanut butter and add teeth–pretend teeth made of tiny marshmallows, and then your own–to eat them!	Show a toothy grin. Count your teeth. Talk about a visit to the dentist. Does anyone in the group have loose teeth? Design the perfect toothbrush.
OPPOSITES	Antonyms are words that are opposites. Give the group a list of words and challenge them to find antonyms for each one.	Make a mirror image. Put a blob of paint on one half of a piece of paper. Fold and smooth it gently. Open carefully and let the paint dry.	Have pairs of children stand face to face and ask one to try and mirror the other as she moves.	When opposite poles of a magnet are brought together, the lines of force join up and the magnets pull together. Use magnets to examine these opposites.	August 13 is *International Lefthander's Day*. Use your non-dominant hand to write, draw or eat.
HEAT	Heat is transferred through convection, conduction, or radiation. With a flashlight and a globe determine why we get more radiant heat from the sun in the U.S. in August.	Cold things have slow-moving molecules while hot things have fast-moving molecules. Feel the objects in your room. Are the molecules fast or slow-moving?	When heat moves through an object it's called conduction. Test metal, plastic, and wood to see which is a better heat conductor. See page 138 for an experiment.	Have half the group paint a sunrise and half paint a sunset. Which do you see more of? Which do you like better?	Which surface is more comfortable to walk on in bare feet on a hot summer's day, a cement parking lot or blacktop? See page 138 for an experiment.
COINS	Put a few coins in empty plastic milk containers. Shake them to the beat of a Caribbean tune.	A dollar coin to be issued next year will bear the image of Sacagawea, the Shoshone girl who guided the Lewis & Clark expedition. Find out about her.	New quarters are being minted to celebrate the 50 states. The five coming this year include CT, DEL, GA, NJ, and PA. Find one of each and check them out.	Bring in or ask children to bring coins from other countries. Compare them to U.S. coins. Make coin rubbings using different colored crayons.	Design your own coin. How much would it be worth? What would you call it?
HANDMADE	Paint or draw a mural on butcher paper of a landscape using handprints as the trees, flowers, bird's feathers, rainbow, clouds and bushes.	Make up a secret handshake and teach it to a friend.	Decorate old gloves (or lunch bags with a glove shape drawn on them) to make hand puppets. Tell a story using the different characters on each finger.	Learn a hand clapping rhyme. Practice and see who can do it the fastest.	Have a relay race to see which team can fill a pail with water at the finish first, using only cupped hands to carry the water.
CHILL	Freeze sturdy water-filled balloons. Remove the balloon skin. Do they float? What happens if you put salt on them? How long do they take to melt?	Melting, moving glaciers changed the geography of the earth. Put a chunk of ice on a sand hill and see if the shape of the sand changes.	Glue a plastic ornament inside a baby food jar lid. Add water and a pinch of glitter to the jar. Glue top on with waterproof sealant. Shake the snow globe.	Conduct an experiment to show that water expands when it freezes. Mark the water level in a container. Freeze and see where the frozen level is.	Serve iceberg punch. Put some ocean (blue Kool-Aid) in a large bowl or clean bucket. Add odd shaped ice chunks. How much of the ice is above the ocean?

Olympics Down Under!

It's Olympics time again, but this year the Olympics are being held from September 15 to October 1 because the location is Sydney Australia, where the seasons are reversed. So traditional Olympic dates in June and July don't apply because in Sydney it's winter! The Olympics this time will begin in the Australian spring.

While school-agers are still in the summer program before school starts again, it's a great time to have your own Olympic games, and learn more about Australia.

Kid Olympics

Have an Olympic field day, or spread games out over an entire week. Have relay races, high jump, broad jump, team games like basketball or field hockey, and if you have access to a pool, have swim contests. You may want to throw in some "wacky" games, or games for fun that ensures that everyone comes out a winner. Also, try these three games:

Javelin Throw: Each child personalizes a milk cap or similar object to use as a marker. Give each team an empty cardboard wrapping paper tube to use as the javelin and a tape measure. Each team lines up single file behind the throwing line. Each child throws the "javelin," then marks where it lands with his/her marker. Determine the longest throw.

Shot Put: Give each team a small soft rubber ball. (Nerf balls probably won't work well.) Each team member throws the "shot put" then marks where it lands with their marker. Measure the length of the longest throw.

Balance Beam: Draw a 4 in. X 16 ft. rectangle on outdoor blacktop. Teams create a series of movements that members perform on the "beam." Award points for participation, creativity, and balance.

Trophy Time

Before your Olympic games, have the children make a variety of trophies and medals to be awarded to winners of games. Use recycled materials such as paper tubes, small boxes, yarn, ribbon, makers, stickers, toy figures or small objects, etc. Encourage artistic creativity. Include awards for "Best Sport," "Best Team Spirit," etc.

Aussie Animal Olympics

Help the children make a list of animals that are unique to Australia. The list might include the kangaroo, wallaby, koala bear, duck-billed platypus, and others. Then ask the children to think about what kinds of Olympic events each of these animals might engage in. Have photos of the animals in their natural habitat to spur suggestions.

For example, the kangaroo might do well in the broad jump, the platypus in a swim meet. Let the children draw pictures of the animals participating in the Olympics!

Be Inventive

August is National Inventor's Month. Give the school-agers some time to relax and daydream to come up with ideas for inventions that would make life easier. For inspiration, share the following books with the kids: *Brainstorm!: The Stories of Twenty American Kid Inventors* by Tom Tucker; *Accidents May Happen: 50 Inventions Discovered by Mistake* by Charlotte Jones; and *Inventors* by Martin W. Sandler.

After kids have had some time to reflect on what they would like to invent, ask them to make a diagram of their invention. If materials are available, let them build the invention or create a scale model of it.

Recycled Airplane

Make this pull-toy from recycled materials. Older school-agers can make these for a toddler program. What other ideas can you think of for making toys from recycled materials?

Take a 1 qt. plastic bottle with a handle (bleach bottle). Paint or decorate the bottle to look like an airplane. Insert an old child's thong sandal through the handle to make the wings. Cut four wheels from another sandal. Insert sticks through holes punched into the top and bottom of the bottle and attach wheels to the sticks. Simple!

International Friendships

August is the time of year when hundreds of students come from dozens of other countries in order to spend a year going to U.S. high schools. Your program can help ease their transition into U.S. society by developing friendships with these students. Everyone benefits from creating international alliances.

Find out if the high school in your area will have any exchange students in class this year and if so, let your school-agers provide the services suggested on page 141.

	Monday	Tuesday	Wednesday	Thursday	Friday
AUSTRALIAN OLYMPICS 2000	Find Australia on a world map or globe. Learn 5 facts about Australia. Examples: a country and a continent; mostly desert; unique animals like koala and platypus.	*Aboriginal Art:* Make "bark" for bark painting. Cut up brown grocery bags. Crumple, then smooth out. Brush with watery brown tempura paint.	*Bark Painting:* After drying the "bark" overnight, paint animal or geometric designs on bark with bright-colored poster paints. Dry, then display.	Read *Koala Lu* by Mem Fox. Create "Australian-style" Olympic competitions: crocodile crawl, kangaroo hop, koala climb, sloth saunter, snake slither.	Have an Australian snack. See *Possum Magic* by Mem Fox for ideas such as vegamite sandwiches.
GOOD SPORTS WORLD ROUND	On a current world map, use sticky dots to mark each nation competing in the Olympics.	Make a list of good sportsmanship behaviors like respecting opposing team players, congratulating winners, being gracious in loss. Why is this important?	Write a short paragraph inspired by this statement: "Winning isn't everything, but a winning attitude is!" Who are some pro athletes who exhibit a winning attitude?	Children share their paragraphs, then bind all of them together into a book for the center. Everyone consults on positive title for the Sportsmanship book.	*Media Scavenger Hunt:* Children bring articles and ads about the Olympics to summarize and share. Post on a bulletin board.
FUN DATES TO OBSERVE	August 2 – James Howe's birthday. He wrote *Bunnicula*, *Howloween*, *The Celery Stalks at Midnight*. Pick one to read aloud to kids during quiet time.	August 7 – *Picnic Day* in Northern Territory, Australia. Have a picnic. Include some Australian vegamite sandwiches.	August 8 – Matthew A. Henson birthday. Learn about this important African-American explorer who reached the North Pole with Robert Peary.	August 9 – *U.N. International Day of the World's Indigenous Peoples.* Who are "indigenous peoples?" Share examples. (Any native peoples who preceded immigrants.)	August 10, 1846 – Smithsonian Institution was founded to house cultural, historical and scientific collections in the U.S. Give kids a day to share their collections.
CITIZENS OF THE WORLD	Make posters to welcome arriving foreign exchange students.	Prepare a list of "Useful Things to Know" to give the exchange students. Make it fun; include items like "best place for ice cream," etc.	Host a breakfast or lunch and let foreign students briefly tell where they are from and a little about themselves and their country.	Post a laminated world map and put a sticky dot on each country where the exchange students are from. Use a different color and mark countries the school-agers are from.	Let school-agers imagine what it would be like to live in another country for a high school year. Where would they like to go? Research that country.
BEETLEMANIA	On a field trip, kids look for new or old Volkswagen "Beetles" and call out "*Beetlebug!*" when they spot one.	Supply insect books and let school-agers determine how many different types of beetles there are.	Make beetles by molding plaster-of-paris in plastic picnic spoons. When dry, paint fanciful designs.	Find a patch of flowers and simply sit still and watch. Flowers have lots of insect "traffic." Write down all the different types of bugs you see.	Have a "buggy" singalong. Sing songs from *A Creepy Crawly Song Book* (Farrar, Straus, Giroux, 1993), or old favorites like *There Was An Old Lady*….
MAKE AND TAKE	*Crazy Towers* – Cut cereal boxes into crazy shapes. Decorate with markers or rubber stamps. Cut small slits at edges of the shapes. Slide pieces together at the slits.	*Stick Puppets* – Cut out figures from magazines; trace and cutout cardboard to match and glue; attach to sticks. To make arms and legs move, cut off and refasten with paper brads.	*Salad Spinner Art* – Put white paper plate or circle of paper in the bottom of a salad spinner. Add different colors of liquid tempera paints, put on top and spin.	*Animal Rocker* – Cut a paper plate in half. Glue a small box between the halves so they become rockers. Add cardboard arms, legs, head, and tail to make any animal.	*Hand Plaque* – Pour plaster of Paris into a small oiled pie dish. Press hand into plaster mix until plaster sets. Inscribe name with a nail while still wet and paint after dry.

PLAN YOUR AUGUST ACTIVITIES!

THEMES:

_____

_____

_____

_____

STAFF PERSON

_____

_____

_____

_____

ACTIVITIES:

_____

_____

_____

_____

_____

_____

_____

_____

FIELD TRIPS:

_____

_____

_____

_____

_____

_____

_____

_____

INDEX

NOTE: Italicized entries indicate article titles

INDEX